Gospel Subplots

Story Sermons
Of God's Grace

David O. Bales

Foreword by
Dr. Kenneth C. Haugk

CSS Publishing Company, Inc., Lima, Ohio

Copyright © 2000 by
CSS Publishing Company, Inc.
Lima, Ohio

Scripture quotations are from the *New Revised Standard Version of the Bible*, copyright 1989 by the Division of Christian Education of the National Council of the Churches of Christ in the USA. Used by permission.

Library of Congress Cataloging-in-Publication Data

Bales, David O., 1948-
    Gospel subplots : story sermons of God's grace / David O. Bales ; foreword by Kenneth C. Haugk.
        p.   cm.
    ISBN 0-7880-1584-2 (pbk. : alk. paper)
    1. Story sermons. 2. Sermons, American I. Title.
BV4307.S7 B35   2000
252—dc21   99-055644

This book is available in the following formats, listed by ISBN:
    0-7880-1584-2   Book
    0-7880-1585-0   Disk
    0-7880-1586-9   Sermon Prep

Acknowledgments

After 25 years of writing only a half dozen stories, suddenly I broke out in fiction, seeing plots and characters all around and within me. I owe this happy blossoming mostly to the First Presbyterian Church, Klamath Falls, Oregon, for their inspiring me to minister with my best gifts — one of which is writing. Along the way individuals have encouraged me to write: Dan Farr, Laura Isenhart, D. M. and Louise Jones, Carolyn Zimmerman, Ellie Nicholson, Sherrill Boyd, my brother Jim Bell, my friends Phil Young, David Paap and Ken Haugk. My wife Judy Bales, and our daughters, Katherine, Mary and Lydia, have each given support and criticism for my story sermons.

For these stories I needed advice and it was graciously given by (in alphabetical order): Jim Beggs, Don Boyd, Sr., Don Boyd, Jr., Jack Dow, Glenn Gailis, Bill Ganong, Sr., Ken Morton, Stu Shaw, Bert Singer, and Rebecca Ullman. I remember how thrilled I was to see my name on someone else's book. Hopefully it is a thrill for you too. This is my thanks to you and to God for you.

I owe thanks to those who regularly attend our Informal Worship Service, at First Presbyterian Church, Klamath Falls, and also to First Presbyterian Church, North Bend, Oregon, for listening to and discussing these stories at their summer conference.

Table Of Contents

Foreword

Stories have the power to reach us in ways that merely stating truths or reciting proverbs cannot. The Old Testament prophets knew it. Jesus knew it. Over the centuries the most effective communicators of the Christian faith — whether they were teachers, preachers, or lay persons — have been those that understood the potential of a good story to change lives, and they knew how to tell that story in an engaging way. With this book, Reverend Dave Bales demonstrates that he is one of those effective communicators.

Through this book, you will enter into the lives of persons from several periods of history, from many walks of life. Dave convincingly writes from the viewpoints of a wide variety of people, sharing about their joys and struggles as if he had experienced them himself. The stories will draw you to live in another person's world for a while, to try to understand real life issues from that individual's perspective. You are also likely to discover aspects of yourself in some of the characters you encounter.

More than merely good stories, the pieces in this volume are firmly grounded in solid Christian theology. Dave's background as a biblical scholar is clearly evident. In some of the stories, this biblical basis is very clear; in others, it is more subtle, requiring the reader to stop and think about what is being communicated. This subtlety gives these stories the ability to do more than just share Christian values. The tales in this book will call you to look at your own faith, sometimes in very challenging ways. They invite you to think and reflect on your life journey, providing you with an opportunity to identify and address aspects of your life that may be inhibiting your walk with God. While the stories themselves offer this invitation, the accompanying discussion questions can also facilitate further probing of the message of each story to discover its precepts for faithful Christian living.

Just as I found Dave's background as a biblical scholar extremely valuable when we worked together to develop the *Haugk*

Spiritual Gifts Inventory, I am confident you will also benefit from his insights and knowledge as you study this book. I invite you to turn the pages and enjoy your journey with the people you find here.

Kenneth C. Haugk, Ph.D.
Executive Director Stephen Ministries
Saint Louis, Missouri

Introduction

If it is strange to hear a story for a sermon, it is strange because the church has missed one important fact about the Bible: the Bible has more stories than anything else. It is God's idea from the beginning that the bulk of the Bible is narrative. If over the centuries Christians have become used to sermons being a string of assertions, explanations, or exhortations (with a sprinkling of stories as illustrations), the sermons have not been preached in a manner consistent with how the Bible communicates reality. Most of the Bible is stories.

In the Old Testament stories are even duplicated, as in the books of Kings and Chronicles. Sometimes the same story is told two different ways on the same page — as the two creation stories in Genesis (not to mention the other descriptions of creation in the middle of Isaiah or in the book of Psalms). A story in Deuteronomy Chapter 26 holds a central creed in the Old Testament. The worshiper brings a basket of first fruits to a shrine and repeats the story of faith: "A wandering Aramean was my ancestor; he went down into Egypt and lived there as an alien, few in number, and there he became a great nation, mighty and populous. When the Egyptians treated us harshly and afflicted us, by imposing hard labor on us, we cried to the LORD, the God of our ancestors; the LORD heard our voice and saw our affliction, our toil, and our oppression. The LORD brought us out of Egypt with a mighty hand and an outstretched arm, with a terrifying display of power, and with signs and wonders; and he brought us into this place and gave us this land, a land flowing with milk and honey." Thus, telling the story of what was done to my faith's forebears incorporates me into the faith.

The New Testament also presents God's truth through narrative. But again, one telling is not enough. Matthew and Luke rewrite Mark, then John sets to work and records his Gospel from yet another perspective. But all four Gospels are stories: overlapping, duplicated, redundant stories. If we do not understand God in Christ when the story is told in one Gospel, we have three other editions of the good news to read. Stephen, Peter, and Paul each recount the Christian faith by reporting the stories of God's faithfulness to them and to God's whole people. Sometimes the New Testament story of faith is as brief as, "One thing I do know, that though I was blind, now I see."

The Post-New Testament church continued to recount its basic beliefs through retelling the story of its faith: "I believe ... in Jesus Christ ... conceived by the Holy Ghost, born of the Virgin Mary, suffered under Pontius Pilate, ... crucified, dead, and buried; he descended into hell; the third day he rose again from the dead; he ascended into heaven, and sitteth on the right hand of God the Father Almighty...."

The stories in the Bible are truth with legs. The truth walks across the Bible's pages and we see what happens when people rebel, regret, repent, and are redeemed. Then, after we slosh through life with those shown in the Scriptures we are prepared for the non-narrative writing of theological statements or commands. But the non-narrative material in the Bible explains the narrative and the non-narrative material is absurd without the narrative.

Story sermons do today what Jesus did in his stories — they sneak up on people. Listeners can ward off moral exhortations, and they become resistant to three points, a poem, and a prayer. Intellectually they can parry with information doled out in a series of reasoned arguments. But stories win us over before we understand what is going on. Stories quietly tip the scale of our minds toward agreeing with God's graciousness.

Jesus did not use stories for everything (too many stories become a rhetorical avalanche burying listeners in their emotional responses), but Jesus regularly used stories to portray God's funneling of eternal love into this world. If Jesus' stories do not slice deeply into our souls, perhaps it is because too often we have heard them moralized, or maybe we need to see them in modern dress and to hear them in contemporary language.

Jesus makes us think about God's actions among us by telling short, deceptively simple stories. Jesus' story-sermons (his parables) are meant to unnerve us. They are not soothing bed-time fare. Jesus throws out his parables to attract and challenge us with the good news. Jesus' parables jerk us out of the usual, turn us around, and make us look at ourselves, God, and the world in utterly fresh ways.

When hearing one of Jesus' parables we enter into its world. We don't just grasp Jesus' story, it grasps us. Jesus hooked people with stories, and whether they liked what he said or were enraged by it, they certainly remembered it. Jesus' parables are time bombs. They go off after we've thought about them for a while. They are depth charges exploding within us when we understand in the depths of our lives that God's actions are not fair, they are gracious — to others and to us.

Jesus uses stories to force us to look at what God is doing right now. Notice that Jesus does not gather a crowd and read the Old Testament to them — no one in the New Testament does such a thing. Nor should we. What has been written before is not enough. Jesus' stories insist that we encounter God today; thus in Jesus' stories God becomes contemporary to us, and we experience (and re-experience) God here and now.

Mostly, Jesus' parables force us to decide for or against God's venture in Jesus; for or against a God who forgives when forgiveness is not warranted; for or against a God who keeps giving people second, third, and fourth chances; for or against the God and Father of our Lord Jesus who would raise him to new life, and include us also in Jesus' resurrection.

The proof that God speaks powerfully to us through stories cannot be understood merely by thinking about stories. Take the time before Christmas to read aloud Matthew Chapters 1 and 2 and Luke Chapters 1 and 2 to hear and see again what God has chosen to communicate to us through a story. The God who lived among us in Jesus Christ is the God of new beginnings, the God constantly present with us, and the God who shall bring all things finally to an end. At the beginning of Lent or Holy Week, turn to the Gospels, and read the stories of Jesus' last week of life. On the pages of the New Testament is the master story of God genuinely in our midst, loving us, dying for us, rising to new life for us. No tricks with smoke, mirrors or selective video editing, God here. The greatest story ever lived. A story that demands retelling.

11

* * *

About these stories: They were written to be read aloud, as some people said (approvingly), "performed" aloud. Certainly the folk in the Bible told their stories expressively. Can anyone imagine Jesus speaking a parable in a monotone? Thus, read these aloud and read them with all the interpretive abilities you have — to the glory of God.

About the Discussion Questions: Assume that each question, where applicable, is followed by the further questions: Who? When? What? Where? How? Why? Can you give an example?

Text: Isaiah 21:11-12

Chapter 1 — Advent

Watchman, Tell Us Of The Night

To strangers the plains of Eastern Montana seem barren, especially in late autumn. The horizon appears endlessly flat, and only occasionally above the plain a low row of hills pushes up — sometimes just a large bump of ground. Homesteaders built a small frame church upon one such rise, and it has stood since 1912, spared prairie fires, but not free from time's toll. For safety the steeple was removed and the roof sags six inches in the middle of the span. But every season and every week, worship is held.

With a crisp wind promising early winter, Sunday morning clatters with the sporadic arrival of cars and pickups. Each arriving worshiper first sees the same person every Sunday. Beside the church's front door an older woman stands facing the wall. She is there before anyone comes. When the last has gone she finally leaves. Each worshiper, before entering the door, walks over and touches her. Adults pat her on the shoulder, sometimes whispering, "God bless you, Fern," or, "We love you, Fern." Children, just learning this ritual, touch her hand before they enter the house of worship. The woman hardly moves and never speaks. A gust of wind rocks her. No snow yet, but it's coming. She steadies herself and tugs her collar tighter around her neck.

"Thank you for the touch. Thank you for the hug. I nearly burst to tell you, but I can't. Bless you too, Sarah. Thank you, God, for these people. Thank you that they can go in those doors, and walk to their pews, and sit to pray and stand to sing. Thank you for them; because although I know I am welcome, I cannot enter.

"I see the little communion table, right in the center, 'Do This In Remembrance Of Me.' I feel the tattered green hymnbooks. I'm old enough to remember the smell of smoke from the wood stove. Now they have an oil furnace, but it goes out once a winter. I recall the stained glass windows by heart, and which ones are cracked. I

13

can feel the flooring giving way slightly and creaking under each step. I remember the baptisms, weddings, and —

"We brought Dwayne here to be baptized. Our first, for whom we shed our tears and exercised all our fears. We were too poor to afford corrective surgery for his cleft palate, and I was so young. I didn't know how to raise a child, barely how to diaper one. I spoiled him terribly. He was a terror to the neighbors, and I thought he would be the most insufferable man on the plains.

"Thank you, God, for their song: 'Come, Thou Long Expected Jesus.' What better to sing in the cold autumn?

Dwayne grew to be the most gentle of people, kind, sensitive. He loved conversation. Not talk. He loved conversation. He listened to and was affected by others. He asked questions and wondered about how other people experienced life. He helped with Noanie and Lawrence. And when Wyman abandoned us, Dwayne became more a father to them than a brother.

"The silence means they're praying. Thank you, God, for their prayers. I still sway to the rhythm of their prayers, as you are glorified and beseeched. They honor you and request your help. I know they pray for me also. You know how it was when Wyman left. Noanie, Dwayne's long-legged little sister with her big knees and sunken eyes — she was always skinny and awkward and quiet. Only Dwayne could get her to talk much. She asked night after night when her daddy would be back; but what he said that frigid autumn night gave me little hope we'd see him again.

"Not many people would pay to have their laundry done, but I sought them out and washed for them. I worked on the ranches and in the ranch houses, cooked and cleaned, birthed, branded, castrated, and injected calves. I worked for the county, repairing roads. I painted houses a few summers — all the while three kids I couldn't watch or hold or help with their homework and could barely provide for. Dwayne was not only father for the other two, he was his own father.

"Then Dwayne was gone. Almost as though it was two hours from when he was drafted and he was gone. Seemed I was never home in the days he was preparing to leave. I was working one and a half or two jobs, and he was home with Noanie and Lawrence. I

14

was a stranger to my own children, and found that when it was time to say good-bye to Dwayne I didn't know what to say, nor did he. We gave him away at the Greyhound station, and only saw him twice again. He is part of the vegetation in Vietnam, blown to so many pieces they didn't try scooping him into a bag.

"They're singing, 'O Come, O Come, Emmanuel.' I'd love to join the song. I know the words by heart; but I can't speak when I come here. I can't speak and I can't enter. It's not just that Dwayne's memorial service was here. As terrible as it was for me to walk into this building again, I did, because his body hadn't been here. But four years later Noanie left, silently, one day when I was cleaning rooms at the motel. She slipped out, she with her deep eyes and thin legs, she with her silence and her pain. She phoned a couple times a year and came back three times. But she was addicted by then, and when last she came home, as hard as it was to believe, she was half the weight of when she left. I carried her to her own bed to die; and she was tended by church-folk as much as by me.

"It was after her funeral I discovered I couldn't walk into the church. I can lay my hand upon this cold, peeling paint. I know the dimensions of the structure out and in. I can count the ceiling beams in my sleep, and could pick out the color of the faded kitchen linoleum on a color chart. But I have never been able to go into this beloved building again.

"I knew nothing to do but to work more and try to keep Lawrence at home, but Lawrence — the angry one, Lawrence, the walking prison, the one I knew least, Lawrence who turned pale when anyone asked him what he was going to be when he grew up, Lawrence who seldom made sense with what he said or did — Lawrence at least told me he was leaving. A week after Noanie died Lawrence up and said he was going to the city to find his dad.

"I said, 'You won't be finding him anywhere. He's long gone.'

"He said, 'Maybe I won't find him, but I'll look for him.'

"And that chilly autumn evening he was out and gone and the house was death-still and vacant as it hadn't been for thirty years. And the Sundays and Mondays keep rolling around regularly and I come here and then I go to work. Nothing else to do, but stand here on Sunday and work on Monday, and wait. Wait for Lawrence to come back.

"They sing of Advent. 'Watchman, Tell Us of the Night.' They sing it for me. It's dark and it's autumn, and the nights come earlier and the snow has already made a couple wild passes at the plains. You don't have to tell me of the night, God. Nothing you must say to me. But I am glad you listen.

"Thank you for your people inside. Their way was mine for half a century, but I can't join them now no matter how many times I imagine myself inside with that tiny, joyful group of neighbors. Bless them, as they worship for me. I'll stand here with you and wait. I'll let them worship on my behalf. And I'll stand here and wait on their behalf. I'll wait in autumn's darkening days, either for Lawrence to come home or Jesus to return, whichever comes first."

* * *

Receive the blessing: May God Almighty, Father of our Lord Jesus Christ, giver of the Holy Spirit, bless you where you worship and where you wait, where you suffer and where you serve, now and forever. Amen.

Discussion Questions

Text: Isaiah 21:11-12

1. What immediate responses do you have to the story?

2. If you could have a conversation with one of the characters in this story which would you speak with and what would you ask or say?

3. Do you identify with any character in the story?

4. What is your earliest memories of Advent and what did it mean to you then?

5. What does Advent mean to you now?

6. What do you most eagerly wait for?

7. Without naming anyone, have you endured much "private suffering"?

8. What is your most earnest prayer?

9. In that Christ rewrites our lives, what from this story would you like to have happen in your life?

Text: Matthew 2:1-2

Chapter 2 — Advent

Four Years Not Quite Too Late

At the Christian Endeavor Christmas party, 1948, the group of high school students had sung Christmas carols for half an hour, but before they exchanged gifts Brooks Webber stood to speak. Twenty-four years old, he was well liked by the students from his own church. But Christian Endeavor was students from many churches and denominations. He moved to the podium, cleared his throat, and said, "Good evening. I'm Brooks Webber and I want to share some information about Christmas from the first two chapters of Matthew's Gospel."

A couple of girls in the front row became attentive. A boy in the back, Brooks' neighbor, listened. The other 35 were a little quieter in their conversations. He said, "I've been studying the first two chapters of Saint Matthew's Gospel, and Mr. and Mrs. Bowman asked if I would add my thoughts about Christmas to your party."

A dozen more students dutifully turned to listen. Brooks said, "We only read of Jesus' birth in Luke and Matthew, and both those Gospels tell it differently. To learn all about Christmas you have to read both. But tonight we'll focus on Matthew."

His voice was unsteady, which did not gain him listeners. It also did not help that he spent ten minutes explaining the genealogy in Matthew. Those students who had given their attention remained quiet, but one was playing with her pony tail, another was tapping his knee with his comb. Mrs. Bowman stood at the side of the group shushing three girls. Mr. Bowman took two boys from the room and scolded them. Brooks started to explain Joseph's dream, then said, "I guess I'll tell something different about Christmas. I should have told someone years before. If it's okay, I'll tell you about Christmas four years ago.

"Four years ago I was in the Second World War. Any of your fathers in the war?" A dozen hands went up. "Remember V-E day?" All hands rose. "Remember V-J day?" All hands rose.

"Well, before we got to those victories there were years of fighting. I was in Luxembourg at Christmas, '44. I was an infantryman in the Battle of the Bulge. Heard of that?" Half the students raised their hands.

"Hitler threw against us his last flurry of evil. Two hundred thousand Germans with 600 tanks surprised us and the fighting was fierce through Christmas. It was cold, snowy, and foggy. First we retreated, but we never really knew which direction the front was. On Christmas Eve the fighting was still murderous. Plenty of us were cut off from our outfits, and we latched onto any soldiers we found, and made our own squads.

"At dusk I dashed through a jumble of briars and tumbled into a shell hole with two other fellows. None of us were from the same outfit. We were freezing and scared and tired — we'd been running or fighting for a week. We had no idea what was going on around us. Rifle fire and artillery had sounded from every direction. We thought we had support on our right and hoped we had it on our left; but we weren't sure, and we didn't dare leave the hole to find out.

"We were at the edge of a field — maybe 25 acres, not quite flat. Out front was the debris of war: a dead horse, a blown-up German half track, and an American Jeep on its side. Smoke still curled from inside the half track, muddying the air. Occasionally we'd see flashes from artillery shells, but the fog deepened and with the dense cloud cover the night became completely black.

"Shaking with cold and fear, we introduced ourselves. We might have given our last names, but I was so tired I forgot as soon as they told me. I just remember Stan and Virg. We waited a few hours for an attack, but when none came we pulled out what food we had and shared. Not much for Christmas Eve dinner in 'K' rations.

"We waited three or four hours but no attack came. Only then did we talk. We whispered what information we had, where we thought we'd been, what we supposed was going on. We knew

20

about the executions at Malmédy and we'd heard about German troops dressed in American uniforms, but none of us had talked to anyone in the last three days who had even talked to anyone who had talked to anyone who knew what was going on.

"It was around midnight that Virg started shaking and crying. Just came on him. We had started our turns at lookout. He was first. I was dead asleep. When I woke my heart was pounding so hard I thought it would break my ribs. Virg had cracked up. I was between him and Stan so I was trying to calm him, but I was so numb I could hardly move. He cried and shook so hard he vomited. Stan was better at quieting him than I. I don't remember exactly what we did, shook him and hugged him, and Stan started talking about Christmas. He chattered about Christmas when he was a kid, where his family visited and what they ate. Then he talked about being with his fiancée's family the Christmas before. 'Remember last Christmas, Virg?' he asked. 'Where were you last Christmas?' He got him to answer, if only with a few grunted words. Then he went on, 'Let's tell about our best Christmas present — you wanna' do that, Virg?'

"We were desperate and tired, and, I suppose, foolish. But Stan said, 'Here, have a cigarette.'

"Stan struck a match low in the shell hole, and Virg bent to light his shaking cigarette. We all bent low to light our cigarettes, then made sure to keep them low. By the light of the match we could see how bad Virg looked. The three of us were all on lookout now and Stan went on with his Christmas idea. 'I'll start,' he whispered. 'I was nine. My folks gave me a toy tractor with a whole set of farming equipment: a mower, I remember, that attached right to the side of the tractor, and a plow and a disk and harrow. I can't tell you how many acres I farmed with that equipment.'

"Virg chuckled, so Stan said, 'How about you, Virg, what was your favorite Christmas present?'

"Virg said, 'A striped T-shirt. Came in the mail from my uncle's cousin. Strange that we exchanged gifts. I wore that shirt until it was a tight, tattered web.'

"It was dark, but in the slight glow of the cigarettes I could see them looking toward me so I whispered, 'It was a baseball. I was

21

probably eleven. Thirty degrees below zero in Wisconsin and I got a baseball for Christmas. First new one I'd ever had. So my brother and I went out to play catch, and after a few minutes it flew over my head and into a huge snow drift. We thought we could dig it right out, so we dug in with our bare hands and baseball gloves, shoveling around in the fluffy snow. Took us twenty minutes and then we had to hold our hands in the oven half an hour to thaw out. Until now that was the coldest I'd ever been.'

"We whispered more about Christmas and we calmed down. Then I took the lookout alone while they slept. I was between two unconscious men I'd just met, my elbows propped on frozen briars as I gazed across the field, then right and left, and turned around and peered behind us also. The place smelled of burning rubber, decaying flesh, vomit in the hole, and probably blood. My clothes smelled like that for weeks, even after they'd been washed.

"But it was in that frozen, stinky hole that I looked out and saw the sky clear, ever so briefly. Across the field a small piece of sky opened for about half a minute and I could see a tiny patch of stars. As I looked toward the stars and sighted over the German half track, I could barely see a cross on the side of it. Never thought about the fact that German armor had crosses. That's what overwhelmed me. I noticed the stars in line with that dirty cross. There I was on Christmas Eve, with a cross in line with a star, and I was overcome with God's presence — as though all around me the air was warm and pushing in upon my body. Starting at my feet, I could feel the pressure pushing up till in less than a second it reached my head. I was seeing the star of Bethlehem and the cross of Calvary at the same time. I felt all the pieces of life and existence unite in that frozen field in front of me and I felt as though God was glowing all around me.

"I could not budge. If half the German army had attacked, I know I could not have moved or spoken. I was rigid, for probably ten minutes, then kind of like waves, the experience would come back over me and I'd go through it again. I prayed as never before. I confessed my sins, and I promised God I'd tell Stan and Virg about it first thing in the morning. I promised I'd tell everyone I met.

22

"But the morning came and though I had the words at the back of my throat fifteen times, I just could not start talking about what happened. I suppose they thought I was cracking up too, because I could not string together a half dozen comprehensible words. By noon Christmas day we were relieved, and a lieutenant directed us to the central staging area. The three of us left immediately. By that night we were going our own ways, and within 24 hours I was back with my outfit and eating hot chow.

"All Christmas day I thought about what God had done for me the night before. For days and weeks, even until the end of the war in Europe, I was trying to find a way and a time to tell someone, but I could never force out that first word."

Brooks had spoken jerkily through his story. But now he paused too long. All of the students were silent. Most leaned forward. They waited for Brooks to say what he so obviously needed to say.

"If I had managed to talk to anyone four years ago, I would have concluded that Christmas, and what God did for me at Christmas, is the way that God loves us right here in the real world. And that is true. But I did not get around to telling anyone, and so I have come to believe that Christmas means more than that. Christmas means that when we do not keep our promises very well, or when we do not keep them at all, God still does.

"This is not what I planned to say tonight, but I think this is also what the first two chapters of Matthew tell us. At Christmas God keeps his greatest promise. Thank you for listening, and Merry Christmas."

Discussion Questions

Text: Matthew 2:1-2

1. What immediate responses do you have to the story?

2. If you could have a conversation with one of the characters in this story which would you speak with and what would you ask or say?

3. Do you identify with any character in the story?

4. When you were a child what was your favorite Christmas gift?

5. As a child, where did you usually celebrate Christmas and with whom?

6. What has been the most difficult Christmas for you to endure and why? Have you lived through a crisis Christmas?

7. How has your understanding of Christmas changed in the second half of your life?

8. If you were going to summarize what Jesus' birth means, what would you say?

9. In that Christ rewrites our lives, what from this story would you like to have happen in your life?

Text: Luke 2:1-20

Chapter 3 — Christmas Eve

The Revolutionary In Bethlehem

In the seven hundred and forty-seventh year since the founding of Rome, in the province of Judea, a man and woman ascended the slope to the hamlet of Bethlehem. When they saw the first Roman soldiers at the town's entrance, the couple stopped and the woman readjusted her weight upon the donkey. Then again they journeyed slowly up to the cluster of square houses on the top of the low ridge.

They came to register for the tax evaluation census ordered by Publius Sulpicius Quirinius, legate of Syria. Two auxiliary troops, javelins in hand, swords on hip, inspected every traveler into the city. While the woman sat on the donkey silently looking down, the man pointed out that she would soon have a child. The soldiers saw the humility expected in the presence of Rome's soldiers and waved them by.

Bethlehem was overflowing with people — even the flat rooftops covered with sleeping mats. The man inquired at a few houses and asked some cameleers and donkey-boys, but each replied that no lodging remained. Finally, someone mentioned the caves outside the town which sheltered sheep. In the dim light of dusk the two walked stooped into a cave. The woman looked around quickly and spoke with a tight voice, "I was so frightened by the guard. If he searched us ... "

"I was frightened too, Deborah, but he didn't. Give me the sica."

Deborah reached under her clothing and pulled out a bundle of rags which wrapped the sica, a curved dagger.

Yarib received it and placed it in the belt under his tunic. He was one of the insurrectionists whom the Romans called Sicarii, named for the small knives with which they assassinated their opponents.

"But I'm still glad I came with you," Deborah said.

"Well," Yarib sighed, "your idea of hiding the sica and pretending you were pregnant kept us alive. If the soldiers saw us turn back when we sighted them, they would have chased us."

Deborah held her husband. "I told you when you tried to leave me in En-gedi that when you love someone, you cannot be apart."

Yarib said nothing. Regret it as he may, he had made up his mind only the day before to let Deborah accompany him. She convinced him that his part in the insurrection would be concealed better by traveling with a woman. Now he must hide her.

Deborah lay down in a crevice on the side of the cave and Yarib covered her with their extra clothing. He stacked limestone rocks in front and scooped dirt into the gaps between rocks. Yarib left to tie the donkey elsewhere. As he led it along he wondered if every Sicarius was following his sworn duty.

The Sicarii were the most militant of the groups resisting the Romans. They hated Roman statues. They would not handle, or even look at, a Roman coin with a human image on it. They opposed Roman taxes and the double blasphemy of counting God's people, because the census would set the amount of tribute Judea must pour into the Roman treasury.

Yarib had been recruited by the Papa Sicarius Mishael Bar Calphi. A huge, robust man, the old women sang a ditty about Mishael that he could talk you out of a sneeze, laugh away your indigestion, then steal your eye teeth.

"The Romans are just like the Greeks," Mishael exhorted Yarib. "Sure the Romans construct giant buildings, but only so young men can run around naked, study philosophy instead of the Scriptures, and learn twenty ways to swindle their countrymen." Yarib never questioned Mishael Bar Calphi. Mishael would quickly gasp another lung-full and continue: "The revenue from this holy land should not leave its borders. Besides," he added, as though the clincher for any half-persuaded revolutionary, "when we burn the archives, record of your debt will be canceled. The land you've worked for five years will be yours."

Yarib was convinced. At the next meeting Mishael brought his twelve disciples to worship. Kneeling, they swore to fight to the death. Yarib hardly had time to think before he heard himself chant the oath with the others. From that moment he believed his status with God depended upon keeping his vow to kill Rome's soldiers.

Now as Yarib tiptoed through the alleys of Bethlehem, he was determined to carry out his vow. The opportunity almost stepped on him. The sentry had been relieved shortly after dusk. Yarib had his sica drawn when the sentry stumbled into him in the alley. Yarib plunged as the soldier jumped and twisted away; but Yarib struck him in the thigh, and as the man fell, he said, "Claudia." Yarib hesitated at the name; but in disgust he assumed "Claudia" must be a prostitute.

He had no time to think further. A second soldier rounded the corner and stumbled upon his writhing comrade. Yarib turned and ran. With no spear or armor he could run fast. Still, the soldier was strong and stayed near, yelling curses. Their feet echoed in the narrow streets; and then like a falling star, the javelin flew by Yarib's head, scraping an arch of sparks against a wall. Yarib plunged between the irregular houses, up steps, and around a well. Finally he was free of his pursuer, yet he heard the garrison being called out.

If it were not for Deborah he would go back and fight. He took a long circling route to the cave, diving behind one rock to another, wondering if the rebellion would go as planned. His attack on the sentry was the beginning. By fomenting trouble in Bethlehem, Rome's auxiliary legion would dispatch troops from Jerusalem south. Similar skirmishes in Jericho and Modein would scatter more Jerusalem troops east and north. Then Mishael Bar Calphi and the nine others would make their bold stroke in God's holy city. With the Roman troops depleted at Jerusalem, but before more arrived from Caesarea, they would assassinate King Herod and lead the citizens in revolt. Even if the population of Jerusalem did not help, Mishael said, God would perform his greatest miracle and defeat the Romans without human aid.

Yarib was breathing hard as he crawled between boulders. His knees were ripped and bleeding. But he had not been followed. Entering the cave he whispered, "Deborah," knowing she could not hear him. Before he had had no time to be frightened; now fear flooded him. He wildly uncovered the alcove where his wife lay hidden. He kept whispering, "Deborah, Deborah." Just before she answered it struck him: Maybe "Claudia" was the name of the sentry's wife. Yarib and Deborah clutched one another atop the pile of stones that had hidden her.

"Are you all right?" she asked.

"Yes, but the Romans have one lame trooper."

Deborah did not reply. Yarib said, "If we all keep our vow the revolt begins in four days, and in a week there will be more light in the world, and fewer Romans. God will honor our war and establish his final kingdom."

The two sat now, holding hands. Their hearts slowed and their breathing quieted. After a long silence, Deborah spoke, "Yarib, I thought of pretending to be pregnant, because I am."

Yarib could not have been more shocked if a mountain had tumbled on him, or more pleased if every Roman legionnaire had drowned in the Mediterranean. He could barely see Deborah in the dark but he held her in front of him, hands on her shoulders. "Truly?"

"Yes."

"Oh, Deborah," he squeaked, grasping her tightly. In his mind he saw infants with mothers by lamp light, and fathers teaching children games. He saw the respect the village showed those who had strong sons, and himself growing old with grandchildren who asked to hear again the tales of the revolutionary war. "The revolution," Yarib said. "Great God, the revolution! We must keep the Romans from this cave."

Instantly he was hiding Deborah again. This time he spent more effort for her safety. As he piled rocks in front of her the two parents-to-be almost giggled, "A baby ... probably a boy ... of course a boy ... but maybe a girl ... all right, a girl ... yes, I love you too."

With Deborah safe and prepared to let herself out if he were not back in two days, Yarib left to search for a place for himself. If he were discovered and executed he could bear it, knowing Deborah was safe and they would have a child. Yet now Yarib was not so willing to die. He wanted to live, even if he did not own the field he farmed. He wanted to care for Deborah and children and take them to Jerusalem to worship in the great temple.

He crossed two gullies below the town and rounded a small shoulder on the ridge. No moon shone, but the sky was clear and what seemed the opening of a cave proved to be just that. The smell of sheep was fresh, but it was empty.

Yarib felt for an indentation in which to conceal himself. On one side he found where shepherds had hollowed out the limestone for a feeding trough, and opposite this he discovered a low overhang which could hide him if enough rocks were piled in front. He was hardly covered when he heard voices and through a small slit in his defense he saw a torch stuck into the mouth of the cave, then the body of a Roman soldier, last Yarib saw the sword in his other hand. A second torch appeared, a second soldier, a second sword. Outside a strong Latin voice yelled to the two men. Neither soldier spoke. Each peered with his torch into every crevice. The larger of the two moved towards Yarib, slowly, closer. Tiny slivers of orange light pierced Yarib's chamber. Directly in front of Yarib the soldier turned and continued to search to his left. Then without a word, the two exited the cave.

Yarib's head was pounding. At each heartbeat he feared his head would burst his ears. For half the night he lay in his stone enclosure never wholly able to calm his fear. His body would shake though his mind was quiet. Every time his body's convulsions ebbed, his mind compiled an unending number of methods by which he and Deborah might be executed. Just as he began to pray, two more voices upset him. A dim oil lamp with two wicks entered the hollow. The man holding the lamp helped a young woman. The woman moaned and held her large stomach. "Oh, I need to lie down."

"Here, Mary," he said as he perched the lamp on an outcropping. "Lie here. I'll cover you."

"Thank you. I kept wondering if we'd ever get here. I know you're disappointed we don't have a room, but, Joseph, I'm so glad we arrived."

"At least we have warm clothes, a lamp, and plenty of oil."

Yarib watched the couple briefly, then collapsed into exhausted sleep. He knew it was near dawn when he awoke to an infant's cry. Propping himself on his elbow he found a slit to look through. He saw Joseph prepare the stone manger with straw. Mary wrapped the twitching infant in cloths, and laid him there for a bed.

"Jesus," they agreed was his name. At the name, "Jesus," Yarib remembered "Claudia" that the wounded soldier had uttered. Yarib was disturbed to think that maybe Claudia was the sentry's daughter. For the first time he felt guilty about the attack. He wished he and Deborah were home, and he could find a better way to rid the land of Romans. Seeing this new family, violence did not seem appropriate. And Yarib was embarrassed, believing himself to be witnessing something that should not be seen by anyone else.

A bustle occurred outside the cave; but before Yarib could fear soldiers, in came four working men. They said nothing.

"Who are you?" Joseph asked.

One stepped forward, "We're shepherds."

Husband and wife and four shepherds faced one another as though someone else had invited them all and each was waiting for another to explain why.

"What do you want?" Joseph asked again. "The inn keeper said anyone could use these caves. Do you need shelter?"

"No," another man said. "We're looking for a child."

The third shepherd added, "We've seen angels tonight, lighting the sky with songs about a savior."

The shortest among the shepherds stepped up and said, "At first there was one angel and we were terrified; but he told us not to be afraid, that he had great news for everyone about a savior, the Lord's Messiah born today in David's city."

"And that's why we came here," the first man explained. "The angel said we'd find a baby wrapped in cloths and lying in a manger. That's when the sky split with all these angels praising God and saying, 'Glory to God in the highest heaven, and on earth peace among those whom he favors.' "

Yarib was aglitter at the talk of a Messiah. Mishael Bar Calphi was right. Now starts the war in which God saves his people. Yarib was ready to dig himself out. But he winced at the word "peace."

The parents brought the shepherds to the infant in the manger; and they talked more of the peace expected through this child. "Peace" struck Yarib as hard as a sword. He was not preparing for peace, but war. Yet in the presence of this gentle family and these joyful messengers, peace seemed so clearly to be God's purpose. Yarib believed what the shepherds said, and at the same time he was in turmoil over his assault upon the soldier. He felt covered with shame for his violence. But he did not know what to do. He wished he could grasp for a way out of his guilt as easily as he could throw aside the rocks behind which he hid.

He began to pray — for himself, for Deborah, for their child, for the child Jesus in the manger, for the wounded trooper, for Claudia (whoever she was) — that sometime, some way, he could make up for what he had done, although he had no idea how. As he prayed he trusted the shepherds' message and the good news of the message grew within him — this child, this helpless child, was to be the promised savior. He asked God to save him, not merely save him from his guilt and the consequences of his deed, but save him for a new life — for peace.

He had not decided what to do about the injured soldier, but he knew that the next day he would crawl from his cave to live for peace. However he would do it, he now had the power of peace in his heart.

Now, near the infant Jesus, Yarib, one of the Sicarii, slept again. That night in his chilly crypt he had made a new vow that wherever he went or whatever happened he would do everything he could to bring about God's peace into this world.

Discussion Questions

Text: Luke 2:1-20

1. What immediate responses do you have to the story?

2. If you could have a conversation with one of the characters in this story which would you speak with and what would you ask or say?

3. Do you identify with any character in the story?

4. What is the "nearest" you have been to Jesus' birth?

5. Have you been mistaken about God's purposes, and have you had an experience where you came to understand the meaning of Jesus' peace?

6. Have marriage and children changed your faith?

7. In that Christ rewrites our lives, what from this story would you like to have happen in your life?

Text: John 19:1-12

Chapter 4 — Good Friday

Pilate's Friend

Throughout the ancient world being the friend of the king meant that you trusted the king to protect and advance you as your patron. To be the friend of a king did not mean that the two were partners, companions, or members of the same lodge. The friend worked for the king for unofficial wages, and those wages came as opportunities to share the king's lands, revenues, and booty from military victories.

The relationship of patron to friend went up and down the social scale. You were friend to the one above who ruled, helped, and protected you; and you were patron to the one below whom you dominated, aided, and advanced. All societies in the ancient world had such a structure; no matter whether it was named, it was real.

In the Roman Empire "Friend of Caesar" became official, a title given in recognition of faithful service. "Caesar's Friend" was a distinct rank, an elite fraternity whose members wore a special gold ring with Caesar's image on it. The friend of Caesar could be an ambassador or represent the Emperor in governmental negotiations. To lose such a status meant disgrace, and usually ended in exile or suicide.

* * *

A few years after Jesus was born in Bethlehem, over a few hills to the north another child was born in Jerusalem. No one remembered who his parents were, or how he had survived. He spent his life in Jerusalem, with no memory of parents or relatives, and he did not even know who had named him "Dysmas." His earliest memory was of asking for help. But since he was always close to starvation, thinking of yesterday was a luxury. He only had time to think about today. He knew a few people who had helped him as he raised himself. Yet, for all those who gave him handouts or let him sleep with their animals, he never had a permanent home.

While he was about five he landed upon his life's pattern. He asked what he could do for people. All day he ranged through the markets inquiring if someone wanted help stacking goods, sweeping his stall, or running an errand. Asking to run errands finally put him in the good graces of the chief priest, Annas.

"Need anything today?"

Annas looked down to the urchin pulling on his ceremonial robe. The child was probably ten years old and clothed in filthy rags. For two weeks the boy had met him every day as Annas walked up the temple steps.

"Need anything today?" He asked again, not as a beggar, but as a workman ready for labor. "Yes," Annas answered, "I do need someone to take word to my son-in-law to meet me in the temple. Do you know where Joseph Caiaphas lives?"

"Yes."

"Then run tell Caiaphas to be here after evening sacrifice."

He placed a small copper coin in Dysmas' hand and Dysmas' eyes opened wide. He was off. He dashed down through the crowd that was coming up the temple steps. He ran across the Kidron Ravine, and never stopped until, breathless, he pounded upon the door of the Caiaphas' household. The next day upon the temple steps he awaited Annas, and again Annas found something for him to do.

Annas asked if Dysmas could have a large, ripe apple for after worship. After the morning sacrifice, he met Dysmas standing with his apple. In the weeks and months following he asked if Dysmas could locate choice figs, or find the best sandal-maker. Dysmas never failed.

When Annas was deposed as chief priest he mentioned Dysmas to his son who was installed as chief priest, who handed Dysmas along to the next chief priest who did the same until Dysmas came into the unofficial employ of Annas' son-in-law, Caiaphas. By now Dysmas was about twenty. He had searched Jerusalem for superior goods for Jerusalem's most important families. He could show up at the doorstep of the chief priests or members of the Sanhedrin and ask for work. If they had no work, they would say, "No, not today, but old Ishmael needs help with his olive harvest." If Ishmael did not need him, he would say, "I'm almost finished with the harvest, but I heard that Onias will build his new house after the Feast of Booths." If Dysmas did not find work with Onias, he might hear, "But if you follow the Kidron Ravine and wait around the bend you'll be first to see the caravan arriving today and you could get work with them."

He was so thoroughly conversant with the richest families that other orphan boys asked him where to get work. From his abundance of contacts, he would tell them, and they would show their gratitude, sometimes with a half loaf of bread or a bunch of grapes, or occasionally they brought him something to sell. He never asked where it came from.

By the time Caiaphas was installed chief priest no one doubted who to ask for information among Jerusalem's street boys. Dysmas not only knew the city, he was often the one who spread news about changes among the Sanhedrin or quarrels between the chief priest and the Roman Legate or Prefect.

Having started with nothing he now basked in his limited accomplishments. He was still among Jerusalem's poor, but he was not among the poorest. However, with time to think beyond today, he experienced a strange longing. At first he thought it was for a wife. Roxanne smiled nicely when he saw her carrying water every morning, and her smile made him feel odd.

Yet his longing was not for a female companion, and it was a longing beyond his usual, pressing needs. He desired something other than a roof at night, or a cloak with fewer holes, or food for the evening meal. He realized that he had no person or place to which he belonged. No one looked out for him, although a handful of street boys were beholding to him and fifty-or-so families knew whom to ask for the finest weavers, the freshest meat, the most reasonable perfumers, or which merchants had the best record of getting their ships safely to Rome and back.

He would have settled for steady employment, but he wanted more. He asked himself why he worked so diligently to learn every aspect of Jerusalem yet he remained a pauper. Why try so hard to hear the gossip when, if he were gone, someone else would tell the stories and he would not be missed? He spent his days and a good deal of his nights doing the work of an apprentice friend; and although many people hired him, they handed him on, almost as a slave.

Such thoughts disturbed him in the weeks before Pontius Pilate became Prefect of Judea and came to visit Jerusalem. Dysmas awaited him on the day Pilate's entourage crested the last rise outside Jerusalem.

Dysmas was present whenever Pilate made an appearance in the city. On the third day, after running across Jerusalem three or four times to find out where Pilate would receive guests, Dysmas drew as near as possible among the crowds at the Praetorium to hear the call for further bids on olive oil, rations for the troops, and fodder for their horses. All bids were received, and Pilate said, "Further bids?" Dysmas stepped forward. "Lord, I do not make a bid, but I have valuable information about those you have received."

Pilate, always the practical businessman, gestured with half a smile, "Come here." Dysmas stepped in front of the seated Prefect. "Tell me your valuable information."

"Lord, you will not get lower bids on oil in Jerusalem. The oil merchants have agreed to one price and none will lower it. All you can do is call for bids from another city, Sepphoris or Tiberias. For the rations you won't receive many bids because you have called for them publicly and the chief priests have let out the word that they will flog anyone bringing you another bid. But if you'll allow people to speak to one of your soldiers, there's enough money involved that someone will bid lower. As for the fodder, go to Joppa or Tyre."

Dysmas knew that Pilate would listen merely to demonstrate that Judeans had access to the emperor's friend; but with every word Dysmas watched Pilate become more serious. Pilate stood, said to a guard, "Get his name for when we return next month."

When Pilate returned the next month he did not have to search for Dysmas. Pilate rode through the gate, saw Dysmas waiting, and spoke directly, "Follow us to the Praetorium." Between Caesar's friend and an orphan boy in Jerusalem an association began. Pilate summoned him upon every visit to Jerusalem, asking Dysmas about the mood of the people or for the best buys for Rome. Dysmas helped the Roman secure the full census tax which the Sanhedrin oversaw.

Within a year Dysmas was living in the Praetorium whenever Pilate was in Jerusalem, and the year following Dysmas was traveling back and forth from Jerusalem to the provincial capital at Caesarea as Pilate's representative. He was the first person Pilate asked for advice on merchandise or transport. Dysmas gained weight, had clean clothes, and rode his own horse. He was not bothered that some Judeans distrusted him. He advised Pilate to cooperate with Caiaphas. "Don't steal from the temple treasury. Take from the chief priests after they steal from the people. Keep Caiaphas as the chief priest. Don't depose him and try to find better. Let Caiaphas know you will keep him as long as the revenues continue smoothly."

His advice made Pilate richer than he ever hoped he would be, as the revenues from Caesar's estates and from custom, census, and franchise taxes passed through Pilate's hands to Caesar. Pilate made sure to grab plenty of coins as they rolled by.

Returning to Caesarea after one profitable visit to Jerusalem, Pilate said, "Dysmas, you do well. You have taught me the way of the Judeans." Dysmas beamed over his new status. He now looked beyond today and began to plan for tomorrow. For two more years Dysmas dumped riches into Pilate's lap, lived in whatever palace Pilate occupied, and even knew Pilate's wife, Procla. Standing beside Pilate he listened and gave advice on matters concerning the Judeans. Late that winter as he and Pilate walked by the sea discussing how to wring more taxes from Judea, Dysmas asked, "Lord, since I have proven my worth to you, making you abundantly rich, I ask, as your friend, to receive a tenth of your income." Dysmas saw Pilate's mouth fall open, but Pilate said nothing, and three days later, without enthusiasm, he agreed. "But," he said, "keep the treasure coming."

Which proved harder for Dysmas than he expected, because he no longer lived in Jerusalem, and changes occurred that he did not always know about. Now when he visited Jerusalem he had to

pay the street boys for information, and their contacts were not as
good as his had been. He was earning money, but he was forced to
spend more for information; and now that his advice was sometimes wrong, Pilate forced him to compensate for all income lost
— which was happening more often. Pilate complained to Dysmas,
yet Dysmas could truthfully say, "Yes, my Lord, but I pay for my
mistakes."

That spring during the Passover, Pilate and Dysmas were living in the Jerusalem Praetorium. They speculated about what the
chief priests would do with the prophet Jesus — whom some called
"King." The chief priests had already presented their case to Pilate:
"Jesus has cut our temple business in half. Since the crowds believe him, we can't bring the herds of sacrificial animals or the
money-changers into the temple courts."

It was not surprising to Pilate and Dysmas when the chief priests
and Sanhedrin arrested Jesus and sought Pilate's permission to execute their antagonist. What surprised Dysmas was that Pilate did
not summon him. When Pilate saw Dysmas enter the anteroom he
brushed past him saying, "You stay here," and went out to face the
crowd.

Dysmas was stunned. He could help Pilate in this situation. He
knew each of the Sanhedrin members, whom they deferred to and
whom they dominated. He understood their aspirations and fears.
Dysmas was sure that the matter could be handled so that no one
lost much. Outside he heard the mumble of voices, sometimes raised,
and he identified a word or a speaker, but he could do nothing.

Pilate returned. Dysmas said, "Lord, I could have helped."

Pilate's eyebrows went up. "This is a capital offense, and I can
handle this without your help."

"But they arrested him because they are jealous of him."

Pilate stared at him, "Do you think I am stupid? I can see envy
seeping from these men. Again, this is a capital offense. Do not
advise me on this."

Dysmas was silent as Pilate walked back and forth across the
room, face tight with thought.

"They will press you for a decision," Dysmas said.

"I know they'll keep pestering me, and if they do I just might let them kill this fanatic."

"But why? He hasn't done anything wrong. My street boys say Jesus is a good man and that he has nothing against the Empire."

"Because he's bad for their business, and if bad for their business, then bad for ours."

The crowd outside the Praetorium was shouting. Dysmas said, "This can be worked out. Stand your ground and the priests will back down. There's no reason to kill someone."

"I'm not worried about the priests and Sanhedrin; but why should I let the land populate with deluded saints reaching for lunacy by fasts and visions?"

Dysmas opened his mouth to reply. Pilate said, "Silence," and left to face those condemning Jesus.

Soon Pilate was back, looking more worried. Dysmas could not comprehend Pilate's behavior. "Lord, I hear the people shouting. Did you release Jesus?"

"No, I sent them the brigand Barabbas. Maybe he will quiet them."

"What did Jesus say in your interrogation?"

"Not much of anything."

"Did he tell the truth? If he didn't lie, then why not let him go?"

"We've got Jews camped out all around Jerusalem, every garden, every hillside covered with shelters of pilgrims. This is not the time to worry about truth, but how we can serve the interests of the Empire."

"Lord, will it serve the Empire to condemn someone upon false evidence? Don't let the chief priests write this drama for you. Choose your own way."

"Whose way, mine or yours? Suddenly you're on the side of sanctity. Do you believe this newest moonstruck prophet is in touch with the Jewish God, and that he doesn't long to be admired or obeyed?" But before Dysmas could respond, Pilate turned and left.

Dysmas stood alone in the room where he had become accustomed to advising Pilate. He heard yelling outside, heard the slashing of someone being whipped, and men laughing. Procla entered and looked anxiously at Dysmas. He said to her, "What is the matter with the Prefect?"

She said, "The crowd said that if he sets the prophet free he is not a friend of Caesar. He tried everything, showed amnesty upon another prisoner, and washed his hands of the whole affair."

Pilate entered with five guards. He was surprised to see Procla. She said, "Lord, stay away from the prophet. I have suffered in a dream because of him."

"Lord," Dysmas said, "you can spare this man."

"You are a good thief, Dysmas, but you know nothing of this. The line between blasphemy and sedition is too thin to grasp and hold. The prophet shall die."

"Lord, this is a mistake."

"You make your mistakes also, boy. You forget that my name is stamped upon the coins. My name is carved into the buildings. Maybe I can do my job without you. And if you speak another word, you will see how I make people pay for their mistakes."

Dysmas paused, then spoke slowly, "I think I have seen enough."

Pilate whirled toward his guards, "Who else in the dungeon needs crucifying?"

"One man, Lord, a thief."

"Then drag him out, and take this thief also," he said, pointing at Dysmas. "Nail the Galilean between these two and let's see if Jesus is a better patron to my friend Dysmas than I."

Dysmas had been around Jerusalem all his life; thus he knew what to expect. He carried his cross-piece to the skull-faced hill of Golgotha. He and the two others were nailed by the arms and feet to their crosses. The crowd stood back but Dysmas saw faces of those he had worked for. They yelled at Jesus to save himself. They jeered until the thief on the other side of Jesus took up their taunting. Through his gasps he said, "You're the Christ, aren't you? Save yourself and us." Dysmas had said nothing throughout his humiliation; nothing from the moment Pilate sentenced him, grabbed Procla, and left the Praetorium's anteroom; nothing when the nails spilt his flesh. But he spoke now past Jesus to the thief,

"Don't you fear God, even when you share the same sentence? We are getting what we deserve, but not this man." Then he said to Jesus, "Jesus, remember me when you come as king."

"Truly I tell you,"Jesus replied, "today you will be with me in Paradise."

The suffering hours went by, suffering so great that Dysmas could not think. Then although barely able to open his eyes, in the darkness he saw a soldier approach carrying a huge mallet. He knew what was coming. The chief priests would not want the bodies hanging on the day of Preparation during the Sabbath. The soldier would break their legs so they would die quickly. He saw that Jesus was dead.

He had a few moments left and now he must think. Pilate had made Dysmas prove himself, and then he used him to rob the Judeans. Jesus, knowing nothing about him, had said, "Today you will be with me in Paradise." He did not know much about Jesus and he understood little of what he did know, but he reasoned that a Jesus dead was better than a Pilate living. He did not grasp what Paradise had to do with today; but Dysmas had never had much of a yesterday and he did poorly when planning for tomorrow, so he held to Jesus' words to him, "Today you will be with me in Paradise." Dysmas' last thought was, "Today."

Discussion Questions

Text: John 19:1-12

1. What immediate responses do you have to the story?

2. If you could have a conversation with one of the characters in this story which would you speak with and what would you ask or say?

3. Do you identify with any character in the story?

4. Has your disillusionment in a friendship helped lead you to or deepen your faith in Christ? Has your faith in Christ helped you to endure a broken friendship?

5. What is the "nearest" you have been to Jesus' death?

6. Has there been a time when you believe that Jesus spoke directly to you?

7. Have you felt as though you have suffered with Jesus?

8. In that Christ rewrites our lives, what from this story would you like to have happen in your life?

Chapter 5

The Photograph On The Piano

No matter how careful the nursing and housekeeping staffs, the smell of body fluids hung in the room. Tubes seemed to come everywhere from the patient's body. The blinds were pulled. An older woman and middle-aged woman sat in the shadows beside the bed. Stella Hosworth and her daughter Edna had nothing more to say. The doctor had just left after discussing the ending of life support. He was direct but gentle. The decision was obvious, everyone agreed. Still, although the decision was as much as made before anyone spoke, it was difficult.

The Reverend Henry Hosworth, seventy years and one month old, laid with legs slightly elevated beside his wife and stepdaughter. For six days he had made no response to touch, sight, or sound. Stella said, "It's like he's half been killed. There's no District Superintendent with less tact than Barry Barnes."

"I know," Edna said, "and placed her right hand on her mother's shoulder, her left hand on her stepfather's hand. The Reverend Henry Hosworth, unresponsive to touch, sound, or light for six days, felt his step-daughter's hand and heard her voice.

"Thank you, Edna. I can't mumble a sound or force a limb to move, but I hear you. Thank you for comforting your mother. I want you both to know it's all right. It's all right as never before. Console your mother for me and let her know it's all right."

* * *

I met your mother on the most horrible day of my life. I was 21 and preaching the first sermon in what was to be my church, my first church after I graduated from college. I was never more frightened, nor have I ever preached worse. Yet as I stood at the door of the church dripping with relief that the ordeal was over and greeting the worshipers, up stepped your mother to shake my hand. Here's this short young lady, very pretty, and very pregnant, and I know I have told you dozens of times, but I stretched out my hands and placed them on her stomach. Couldn't resist. All my life around women, five older sisters, and all of them married with children. I've never done it before or since, but I reached out and touched her tummy. You were in there. First time I knew of you and I did my best to touch you.

Stella smiled shyly and didn't seem to mind this stranger patting her. Next to her, and how I hadn't seem him before I don't know, was this giant — red-haired, with teeny, round, thick glasses and a smiling face, one enormous hand wrapped around a miniature Bible and with the other hand he buried my right hand. He was the biggest, reddest, happiest man I have ever met: your father, Garret Swensen.

There was no one like Garret, all about him was joyful. Life fit him, and he fit life. Within a couple of months, for all the struggling I was doing toward a sermon every Sunday, Garret became my friend, as no one in my life had been. I was out to their farm almost every day. Your mother taught school till you were born. Garret said, "If you want to be a farmer, you need a wife with a good job."

I was learning how to farm, but every day was like my first day. I was raised in the city — five older sisters, and my father died when I was seven. I was raised by six women. But working with your father made me a man. I'd be hooking up the horses and they'd never do what I wanted. I'd push and yell, then Garret would speak their names and touch them. He would give that thick-lipped smile and say, "It's all right, Henry."

Later that first year Garret bought a tractor, a used John Deere Model B. I'd spin the fly-wheel, then try to adjust the choke and flip off the petcock on the cylinder. I'd take half a dozen tries to get it started. Garret would say, "Take it easy, Henry. It's all right."

Your father never swore, never missed church or hurried. The nearest he came to hurrying was to go fishing. He loved fishing almost as much as he loved you and your mother. We'd finish milk-

44

ing the cows, then off to the stream — I think you've been back there, a pretty good piece of water on Lawkton Creek. We'd fish and talk. I remember sitting there and asking him why he had such a small Bible when his sight was so poor. He said, "If you're going to read God's Word, why not concentrate *real* hard?"

I always said he asked me everything about the Bible from Aaron to Zion. He'd ask why you had to baptize people; about the different ways that churches celebrated the Lord's Supper; he wondered about people of non-Christian religions. I'd give my opinion. He'd ask, "Is that true, Henry?"

I'd say, "Sure is."

He'd say, "Have you talked to God about this, Henry?"

I'd answer, "Certainly." Then I'd ask his opinion. He'd explain his thinking to me. I'd ask him, "Is that a fact, Garret?"

He'd answer, "A fact."

I'd ask, "Have you discussed this with God?"

"Certainly."

Then we'd laugh and he'd come up with another subject. Your father was the brother I'd never had. When Garret was in worship, his huge face beaming with love for God and love for life, only then did I come near to preaching well. I'd be talking to him, trying to answer the questions I knew he was asking. I'd complain that I couldn't preach well and he'd say, "It's all right, Henry. You're doing all right."

I know you've heard this all your life, but it was that day fishing. We were sitting there — early evening after three days of planting. We hadn't fished those days, so we nearly ran to the creek. We were talking about faith and life and your father's rod snapped with the bite of a whale. Garret sprang to his feet and I was beside him telling him I could see it and it was huge. A Dolly Varden, I think. Must have been eleven or twelve pounds. He fought it for ten minutes when the line snapped and he stood a second looking disappointed. He said, "I'm gonna' get 'im." And with two giant steps he leaped into the creek, feet first, overalls flapping. He was down and up, then down and up again, and I was standing on the bank not knowing what to think or do. Garret yelled, "Come on in,

Henry, the water's just right." So I jumped in, and it was like diving into liquid ice. I came up gasping and Garret laughed until he choked and splashed me and I splashed back and we laughed so hard we almost drowned. We dragged ourselves onto the bank laughing ourselves silly. Then we took off across the field toward the house, hardly able to stand for our laughing, and we burst into the house and blubbered on to your mother, trying to tell her what happened.

That evening at dinner we'd look at one another and laugh. We laughed once a minute all evening. You didn't know what we were saying, but you and your mama laughed too. Every hour the next day I thought about Garret flying through the air in overalls and hitting the water with his long boots. Then on Sunday I had to stand up front and try to preach with this haystack-sized man, arms crossed, smiling at me from the second row.

I have probably fished forty times a year since then and every time I think of your father. No one was better than your father. No one more sincere or faithful. That's why he said he couldn't stand it any more. He signed up to serve in the army in January of 1944. He didn't have to, because of his eyes, plus being a farmer, but by then they were taking almost anyone. He gave up his deferment, and enlisted.

The day he left for the Pacific I went along to the train station. Your mother was holding you. I said my good-byes and left them to be alone. I'll always remember your father walking away, his huge body in uniform. I watched them go, my legs shaking and my intestines cramping. He turned and, with a big smile, waved good-bye, then walked on.

We wrote to him every day and his letters came with the words, "Passed By US Army Examiner." He alternated, addressing his letters to me and writing the letter, "To Henry and Stella," and then to your mother, "To Stella and Henry." But on June 12, 1945, a telegram was delivered, informing your mother that your father was killed 1 June, 1945, on Okinawa.

The next year was almost as hard for me as for your mother. She had to sell the farm, get a teaching job again, find sitters for you. I had to adjust to having no one smiling at me in the congregation, no one to farm with, fish with, talk with, or teach me how to be a man. I had no one to ask me questions about the Bible — not like your father, anyway.

Your mother and I loved the same person, why couldn't we love each other? With the poorest of reasons to get married, we did, in January, 1946. You were three.

We kept Garret's photo on the piano, and talked about him often. We both grieved for him. On our piano he stayed eternally young. Without him I had my usual difficulties preaching. I never preached a good sermon in my life. Thus I was doomed to be pastor in the smallest churches, and never stay long in any church; and your mother had to substitute whenever a school phoned her.

Your mother and I tried hard to make a good marriage. But most difficult for me was when she slipped and called me "Garret." The times decreased across the years, but one night when you were about eight she rolled over in her sleep and said, "Garret." I tried to get back to sleep, but finally I went next door into the church building, held my head against a pillar and wept. Your father whom I so loved, I now also hated.

We also had problems because of my ministry. Every church I served complained about my preaching. The same complaints at every yearly performance review, but in a year or two those who could not abide my preaching had left, and the rest knew that no matter how I tried I could not improve, so they stopped talking about it.

Your mother could remain silent only so long, then her embarrassment would overtake her and she'd try to help. She'd say, "You did it again, got stuck and quoted John 3:16." She was right. I had a professor in college, the most arrogant, cruel teacher who ever instructed future pastors; but one day in class he answered a question by glancing at his Greek New Testament and rattling off this translation, "For God actually loved the world so much that he offered his unique son, that whoever would trust in him might not be wasted, but have boundless life." It's as though each of those words were written upon the chalkboard of my mind; and Stella was right. Every time I got flustered I'd quote it.

Once she said, "Say something funny some time."

"You say something funny and I'll quote you," I said. "I'm not funny. Garret should have been the preacher, not me. He could make anyone laugh." I looked at her wishing she would contradict me and tell me that, no, I was the one called to the ministry; but she said nothing, turned, and left the room.

Those were difficult years. I was fighting with my emotions at home and fighting with sermons at church. I tried sermon magazines, summer courses, books of religious poetry. Behind the pulpit every Sunday I'd look out on the courageously kind, the bored, and the sleeping. Yet Stella and I held together, because we had promised God, but also I think we had promised Garret. No matter what happened, one of us always tried again, and sometimes we laughed. Through those middle years we struggled to an understanding: I was not Garret for her, neither was she Garret for me. At first we struggled to a truce, but the truce grew into genuine peace.

You were the constant joy of our life. Somehow you grew up; and the day we returned from the hospital where we'd seen you hold our first grandchild I said to Stella, "How Garret would have loved to see his grandchild."

"Yes, he would," Stella said. We both glanced toward the piano, but Garret's photograph was gone. I looked wide-eyed to Stella, but she said nothing, turned, and left the room.

These last years we have worried about retirement. I stayed in the ministry because we would only receive a small pension and Social Security. We had no savings. I continued to work after 65, but when my seventieth birthday approached our toothy District Superintendent, Barry Barnes, came to inform me that seventy was mandatory retirement age. I told him I couldn't afford to retire, but he said, "I know, Henry, you're 'just a poor, country preacher.' Well, I agree, I've *heard* you preach." And he laughed in my face.

I tried to convince the Administrative Board to petition the Bishop's permission allowing me to serve longer, but a week later a member of the Board came to tell me they were planning a retirement party for me, inviting parishioners from all my former parishes.

48

That last Sunday was awful — all those people coming because of Stella and me, and I had to preach. I felt I should summarize half a century of ministry. I was humiliated, shaking worse than usual, stuttering, the words on the manuscript blurring. I pretty well quit half way through and said that a dear professor in college translated a phrase of the Bible that well summarized the Christian faith: "For God actually loved the world so much that he offered his unique son, that whoever would trust in him might not be wasted, but have boundless life." Then I quit, and we had a fine party after worship.

* * *

A month later here I am. Yet there's a towering red-haired young man with a ruddy face beaming with glory. He says, "Take it easy, Henry," and he assures me that everything is all right. He says, "God actually loves *you* so much that he offered his unique son, that if *you* trust in him *you* might not be wasted, but have boundless life." He says, "Come on, Henry, let's talk to God about it"; and he smiles and walks away, beckoning me to follow. And it is all right. Please tell your mother. It is finally all right.

Discussion Questions

Text: John 3:16

1. What immediate responses do you have to the story?

2. If you could have a conversation with one of the characters in this story which would you speak with and what would you ask or say?

3. Do you identify with any character in the story?

4. Have you quoted a Bible text to others, only to realize later that you had not accepted it yourself?

5. Have you had a friend whose presence made life and faith easier?

6. Has a friend's death greatly affected your life?

7. In that Christ rewrites our lives, what from this story would you like to have happen in your life?

Text: Luke 10:25-37

Chapter 6

Where The Halls Cross

I have the two best jobs in the world. I teach social studies at Leon Griffith Junior High School (a fairly small junior high) and I am Sunday School Superintendent at Calvary Presbyterian Church (an enormous church school). Each job is my vocation. I tell people that at school they'll find my room where the halls cross. At church they can look but probably won't find me. I'll be in someone's classroom. At each job I practice what I most deeply believe: it's how you see the world that determines how you respond to it. I'll give you an example, actually, two examples.

A week ago today, Monday, I began a unit with my eighth grade class on describing a social world with an image. Last summer I studied "The Social World Through Metaphor" and I figure if adults can think this way junior high students can too. It took about twenty minutes to get the kids into images (word pictures), similes (comparisons using like or as), and metaphors (comparisons without like or as). Then I directed them to their own junior high social world and asked them to describe what student life is like at Leon Griffith. I wasn't surprised that after the class's sputtering start Josh Lampson snatched the idea and ran. "Our social world is like a video game."

"Can you explain that?"

"Well, it's all bouncing off walls and getting out of someone's way because you have to."

"I see."

"Sure," Andrea said, "if you don't you get gobbled up."

"Yeah," Josh said, "but it's not just banging around. You learn the lines and the moves. Everyone knows the game. We know when to zig and when to zag."

The discussion continued as students built variations onto the image of the junior high social world as a video game. I then asked,

51

"Can you change the rules of the game? If you did, what would happen? What change would result in Leon Griffith Junior High being the best of all social worlds? Since how you see your world shapes how you respond to it, I want each of you to write a page using the image of the student body as a video game, and what rules you'd change to make life here better. Keep asking yourself what the new social world would look like and what image you would use to describe it."

Since Laura Epstein and I both planned a similar unit on the social world through metaphor I couldn't wait for our prep period to tell her about the first class. Mr. Tiner, our Vice Principal, came in during our conversation. "Malcom," I said, "Laura and I have been helping our eighth graders reflect upon their social world at Leon Griffith."

"Good, that's in the instructional goals."

Laura said, "But we're doing it a new way. Marian used a different methodology today. Tell him about your first class."

I related the discussion and the image of the video game. "And it was Josh Lampson who came up with the image first," I said. "The other students grasped it and expanded and explained the image."

"That Josh Lampson. He's smart, but he's a pain. I get tired of him being sent to my office. I wish he'd use his brains out of your class as well as in it. I'm sure he has masterminded pennying the faculty door. I get so frustrated finding it jammed shut and having to yank on it, then all those pennies flying out. And from the pieces of conversation I picked up in the hall last winter, I'm convinced he was the one who jammed open the outside drinking fountain and turned the parking lot into a sheet of ice. Remember that?"

"Can't forget it," Laura said. "I'm sure that will be my most vivid memory of the year — driving in that morning to find all the cars backed up, and you directing traffic. You fell, didn't you?"

"That Lampson kid!" he said.

"Malcolm," I asked, "if you were going to describe the social world of the students at Leon Griffith, how would you do it? How do you picture student life here? What's your image?"

Mr. Tiner looked at the ceiling while he thought. "Well, I would say the social world of the students here is like a mile long chicken house in a tornado — all dust and feathers under a giant roar."

I said, "I don't think I'll tell that one to the students." But I certainly remembered it the next day when I took the pupils farther in analyzing the social world of Leon Griffith. "Yesterday in our thinking about the social world here we used an image to describe student life. Today think again with an image — a metaphor or simile — that shows what the social world of the students along with faculty and staff is like."

There were a few attempts, not quite getting it into imagery, but then Josh jerked up in his seat and said, "They're like channel blockers." All the kids agreed, but I didn't understand. "They block the channels we want to watch on TV. Don't you watch TV, Miss Gerhard?" And on they went comparing the teachers to electronic technicians who fiddled with the students' televisions denying them MTV. I gave an assignment similar to the day before: "Assuming that life is pretty much determined by how you see it, how can the students change their perceptions and opinions of the teachers that would make this a better school?" Then I was off to the lounge to find Laura and Mr. Tiner. Laura, of course, was interested. Malcolm read a magazine while Laura and I considered what strategy we could use to help the students view adults more as humans and helpers than as antagonists.

Mr. Tiner put down his magazine. "Want to know how I see the adults here?"

"As a matter of fact, I was looking forward to your opinion."

"The faculty and administration together make up the staff of a concentration camp. We are all prison guards in the concentration camp. By law the kids have to come and by law we have to keep them. If they don't come they are criminals. Thus from morning till night we spend our time and energy guarding potential criminals."

I said I wouldn't share that one with my class either, but an idea was coming clear to me. After school I went to Mr. Tiner's office. He smiled, "Hi, Marian, how's the rearranging of the world going?"

"Fine, but I'm wearing a different hat."

"Okay."

"You know I'm Sunday School Superintendent, and since you went off the board of trustees a couple years ago, you haven't had a formal ministry at the church. Would you consider teaching the Junior High Boys' Class?"

"Gosh, Marian, I've got a lot to do, and I'm with these kids every day. I don't think I'm the person."

"I do. You would do an excellent job. I remember when you were a teacher. And by teaching them on Sunday it might change your relationship with them during the week. Would you at least think about it?"

"Yeah, Marian, I'll think about it."

I wasn't going to give him great gobs of time to think. I waited until I saw him the next morning entering the faculty door. He yanked on it and pennies rolled down the hall. I followed him toward his office. "Have you thought about teaching the church school class, Mal?"

"This is not the best time to request I do something for these boys. See the pennies all over? A gaggle of kids flutter by the door and cover for each other as they stick pennies between the door and jam. With a couple dozen pennies stuck in there you can hardly open the thing. You ought to enter that door sometime. I don't know if I can help these kids. And I think that Lampson boy is the ringleader."

"I don't see it that way."

"Well, Marian, I've been thinking about your images. And I've got one for you. These junior high kids are like goslings all trying to be geese. And the Lampson boy is the silliest goose of all."

I left him at that, but during prep period I promised that if he'd just teach one class I would draw up a lesson plan for him — a simple taxonomy of questions, right out of a social science methodologies textbook applied to a Bible passage — and he wouldn't even have to prepare. If he'd try one Sunday I'd be with him in the room. I guaranteed him I'd keep quiet if he didn't want help, but if he did I'd leap right in and do whatever I could. He wasn't as happy about it as I wished, but he agreed.

What I didn't tell him, and I was pretty sure he didn't know, was that every Sunday Josh Lampson's parents tugged him by the collar to church school. Well, not quite by his collar, but I'd see them arrive, and Josh would look as though he were a conquered warrior with a rope around his neck leading him into slavery.

I met Mr. Tiner fifteen minutes before class, oriented him to the room and schedule, and handed him the Bible study. Then after I named the rest of the boys in the class and noted the ones from Leon Griffith I added, "Josh Lampson is in this class too. You don't mind Josh being in your class do you, Mal?"

"Why no, Marian, a class without Josh would be like a picnic without ants."

I think I detected anger in his voice, but I said, "I need to greet students. I'll be back just before you start class."

I didn't get back as soon as I planned. I was not there for the introductions and niceties at the beginning of class. But I was pleased Mr. Tiner had started the boys into the Bible study and he followed my questions and rephrased them as though he'd taught the class for a decade. The class went a lot slower than I'm going to tell it; but here is a summary of the progression.

Mr. Tiner: "Okay, we've heard the story read while we followed along in our Bibles. Let's make sure we've got the facts: Who are we dealing with here? How many actors are on the Bible's stage? Especially, who do we have at the beginning of the story?"

"A lawyer and Jesus."

"Okay, yes. So let's set them aside for a minute and just look at the story Jesus told him. So who's in Jesus' story?"

"A man who gets mugged."

"Who else?"

"The guy who helps him."

"Who else?"

"The priest and the Levite."

"Yeah, and it helps to know that back then the priest and Levite were like the church's pastor and music director. Now, there's one more person mentioned."

"The innkeeper."

"The scene is set. Let's look at the church's pastor and music director. What are they like? How would you describe them?"

"They want to be cool. They sit in the stands but don't play the game. They're trying not to get involved."

"Now, the guy who stops. Notice what he's called?"

"Samaritan."

"Heard of good Samaritans? This is the fellow who started it all. And in Jesus' time Jews and Samaritans didn't get along. They had feuded for centuries. That's why Jesus uses the Samaritan in the story. So what can we say about the Samaritan? What's he like? What would you name his kind of behavior?"

"He's okay. He does what he'd want someone else to do for him."

"How are the pastor and choir director different from the Samaritan?"

"They don't care about anybody but themselves. They don't think what it would be like to be robbed and beaten and waiting for help. They might be scared that the robbers are still around."

"Why don't some people get involved in obvious human need?"

"Maybe because they've always been treated bad so they don't know any other way to act. Could be they've been beaten so much they just can't think about others. Or they're stuck up. Or they're self-centered."

"But the Samaritan goes beyond the social rules. He's supposed to hate Jews, yet he does a loving thing. Why? Why do some people love beyond their group's prejudices?"

"Their faith helps them. Maybe something God does within them."

"Can Christians today love beyond their social groups, say, blacks and whites?"

"Yes."

"Can Christians today love beyond their nations — like Russians and Americans?"

"Some have."

"How about us? What groups are we in every week? What is our social world?"

"Junior high."

"And within the building of the junior high what are the main social groups?"

"Jocks. Nerds. Popular kids. Druggies. Teachers' pets. Quiet kids. The brains."

"Anyone else? Are you missing anyone in the junior high building?"

Josh had not said much, but he came up with this answer, "The adults: the teachers and principals and all them."

"And how can we as Christians be neighbors, and get along with all the different groups, even young and old?"

Some boys made a few one-syllable responses; but after a time Josh, speaking much more slowly than in my class at school, said, "By treating people right, even when they're different."

Mr. Tiner looked at me. I said, "Mr. Tiner, we need to end class in a minute. Do you want to read the last few verses: 36 through 37?"

Mr. Tiner read, " 'Which of these three, do you think, was a neighbor to the man who fell into the hands of the robbers?' He said, 'The one who showed him mercy.' Jesus said to him, 'Go and do likewise.' "

Class ended with the usual chaos and I was off in three directions at once and just had a half second to share smiles with Mr. Tiner. I was not near him in worship so I did not see him until this morning. I could look down the hall at the faculty door and see him approach. He stopped outside, stretched his hand slowly to the knob, and gently opened the door. He looked down the hall and saw me watching him. He waved, smiled, and went into his office.

From the work I do at the crossing of the halls in Leon Griffith and as the Sunday School Superintendent at Calvary Presbyterian Church I get to see how life works and how God works. Wherever I am I try to see it all through Christ's eyes. I believe that what I have just seen is like Apollo 13 docking the Command Module to the Lunar Module, or the signing of a peace treaty where no one has lost a war, or maybe what I've seen is two wild human males tamed into friendship by their Lord Jesus Christ.

* * *

Receive the blessing: May God Almighty, Father of our Lord Jesus Christ, giver of the Holy Spirit, bless you where you study and where you work, where you suffer and where you serve, now and forever. Amen.

Discussion Questions

Text: Luke 10:25-37

1. What immediate responses do you have to the story?

2. If you could have a conversation with one of the characters in this story which would you speak with and what would you ask or say?

3. Do you identify with any character in the story?

4. Has the Bible "spoken to your condition"?

5. Have you studied the Bible in the presence of people you did not like? (Do not mention names.) What was it like?

6. Has Jesus' message of love, mercy, and reconciliation made a difference in your relationships?

7. In that Christ rewrites our lives, what from this story would you like to have happen in your life?

Text: John 20:23

Chapter 7

Over The Pass

Gerald Carrier's mind was pretty much unoccupied for a dozen miles as he maneuvered the big station wagon around potholes and switch backs. He and his passenger, Richard Kaylen, had been neighbors and best friends for eight years now, and silences did not bother them. Then Richard spoke, "What did you think of Pastor Eric's sermon?"

"Well, I told you first time I invited you to worship he isn't the reason I attend church. I chose the congregation because it's conservative, but he's ignorantly conservative; and he started Catholic bashing again."

Richard laughed, "I thought that would rile you."

"I'm not a Catholic anymore, but I'd go to a Catholic church if it was the only one around. He blabbers about Catholics, but he doesn't know one. He's talking about Catholics 100 years ago, or 500 years ago!"

Gerald's and Richard's sons slept in the back seat. Behind them in the second car were their wives and daughters. The two autos wound slowly down the graveled road through the mountain dusk. A week ago the children had loaded onto a bus at church to attend camp. This morning Gerald and Patti met Richard and Kathleen at camp for the last big day. The four parents inspected the cabins and the crafts, watched the races, prizes and presentations, heard the stories and songs, and joined in the final worship service. Now the two cars proceeded slowly on the gravel road, the women staying far back so not to eat as much dust. Gerald halted at the paved road, made sure he spotted the wives' car behind, and waited for a Frito Lay truck to lumber by before turning left onto the state highway toward the pass.

"I knew what you were thinking," Richard said, "but there's one thing he mentioned I can't shake. He insisted we don't need a confessional, we can confess to one another, and forgive one another in Christ's name."

"You know," Gerald said, "the confessional was about the only thing that really bothered me being Catholic — and I can't say I was a very good Catholic. When I married Patti and agreed to worship in a Protestant church, I didn't know what to expect, but I knew I wouldn't miss the confessional — sitting in a closet talking through a funny little curtain, hoping no one was standing too close outside the door. This is the one time I agree with Pastor Eric. There's no reason to tell a priest your sins. Any Christian can confess to any other Christian and be forgiven by Christ."

"But, Jerry, since you left the Catholic church, have you confessed your sins to anyone?"

"Well, yeah," Gerald answered after he readjusted his seat, "a couple of times, kind of."

"And have you forgiven anyone in the name of Christ?"

"Not actually, though I really think the problem of forgiveness is not so much God forgiving us. God forgives us, period. It's whether we'll forgive ourselves. That's the hard part."

They caught up to the Frito Lay truck, which geared down for the final climb to the summit. Gerald did not try to pass. The road took some dangerous turns, and it was completely dark now, so he would let the big truck lead them. Gerald was ready to put his mind into neutral again, but Richard continued, "If you've only confessed a couple times and never forgiven, then maybe the confessional isn't such a bad idea. How well do Protestants do without it? I can't get away from that part of Pastor Eric's sermon. He says there's no reason for any of us to go unforgiven. We can forgive one another for God. It's really bothered me because of going over this pass already today."

"What do you mean?"

Richard sighed, "I used to maintain this road for the State Highways Department."

"You've never said much about your former job."

"Probably not. This was not the best place for me."

Gerald just drove and waited for Dick to continue.

"In winter I used to drive a sanderplow, and had the twenty miles on this side of the pass as my section. I spent eight hours a night on graveyard shift driving back and forth, plowing and sanding." He paused. "It was ten years ago last winter we had record snow in February, but all of it came in the last twelve days of the month. Our crews worked 24 hours a day. I'd get out of the truck and the fellow from day shift would get in. The seat never got cold. We only stopped long enough for diesel, sand, or repairs.

"It was one of the worst nights, wet snow accumulating two inches an hour, the shoulder poles almost all covered, or knocked down. I know I was tired, and almost hypnotized by the snow in the headlights and the constant ring of the plow dragging on the road. I've thought it through, replayed it in my memory a hundred times, a thousand times, and I can't say for sure if I was looking straight ahead or to the left. I don't know what I was doing when I made a sharp right turn and in half a second there was a man in my lights, and before I could get my foot off the gas I hit him."

Dick gazed silently out the right window. Jerry kept his eyes on the back of the truck in front of him. He did not look at Dick.

"He died instantly. Nothing I could do. I radioed the police, and they came in a while, and an ambulance — though I don't know why so many people responded. The autopsy showed his blood alcohol level was point 35 — a wonder he could stand. He'd been driving down hill — don't know how he got over the pass — and lost control. Must have smacked into both sides of the road until stopping against my side. He couldn't have moved the car without a tow. But he got out and wandered down the road." Dick gazed silently out the right window.

"The whole scene was a nightmare — the body, the lights of all the emergency vehicles, the radios popping off over loud speakers, all the police, and the constant snow, usually blowing sideways, and cars and trucks being waved around us, while I stood there freezing, two officers asking me questions.

"I didn't work for a week. That was standard, during the investigation and review. But when I went back it was on the same section, and I tried to be brave and not say anything about how it bothered me. I would get nauseated passing the spot — a couple

61

times I had to stop and vomit. At least they changed me to day shift so I didn't have to drive by in the dark, and there were only a couple more little snows that March, so I didn't have to go by the place much. Fortunately, that summer I worked on the other side of the pass, and we lived on that side too, so it was easier.

"When the next winter came I asked for a transfer, but that's when we had the reduction in force and no one was getting transferred for anything. All I could do was work or quit, and Kathy was pregnant. I had a different foreman by then and we didn't get along. Thinking back I'm not sure I explained myself very well; but all he said when I mentioned working a different section was that there were plenty of truck jockeys who wanted my job.

"So I was back on graveyard shift and I couldn't sleep, started getting headaches and then a bleeding ulcer. Kathy had Kevin to care for, and I wasn't much help with him or the rest of the kids. It was a horrible winter for me and for her too. When the next winter came, at the first snow I quit. Didn't know what I'd do, but I realized I wanted to move at least 100 miles away, which I did. That's when you got me as your neighbor, you lucky guy."

Jerry did not quite laugh, but he snorted a response.

"Today was the first time Kathy and I have been by the accident scene since we moved. We didn't say anything when we drove by. I'd been anticipating it every curve for 25 miles. I'm sure it gave her the willies too. That's why I didn't eat anything at the dinner. I appreciated you asking what was up, but I couldn't talk about it. Then Pastor Eric did his usual worst, and I was really angry at him, until he talked about forgiveness."

Dick fell silent. Jerry drove on, waiting for Dick to continue, but the silence dragged, both of them staring straight ahead at the truck they followed. Finally Jerry said, "I'm listening."

"I know, but this next corner is the place."

Jerry felt his hands tighten on the wheel and every hair on the back of his neck raise. Jerry was instantly aware of everything around him: the truck ahead with the large red Frito Lay sign on it, mud flaps with orange reflectors, and the small tunnel their headlights made through the forest. In the rearview mirror he saw Dick's car which Kathy drove. He could hear the two boys in the back breathing deeply in the exhausted, happy sleep of children going home from camp. He was especially conscious of the rigid figure to his right. He glanced at Dick as he turned his car sharply around the corner, but Dick focused straight ahead. Jerry looked past him, but there was nothing to see, just the shoulder of the road where a human had died ten years before. They said nothing for at least half an hour. They sat as close as priest and parishioner in a confessional, but without a curtain separating them. Jerry was praying as he had never prayed before, wishing he could help Dick, and telling God he would do what he could but he sure needed some ideas. For miles they drove in silence, until up ahead the truck merged onto the freeway. Dick spoke softly, "You believe you can forgive people for God?"

"Yes."

"Then, would you forgive me for God?"

Jerry looked left to merge onto the freeway. It gave him time to think. He quickly formulated three options, but when he spoke he said, "Dick, all I know about forgiving people for God is what I remember from the confessional. Okay?"

"That will do, I'm sure."

Jerry tried to recall the words which had been said to him every week for sixteen years. He could not remember exactly. It was difficult to concentrate because he was praying so desperately; but he ran through what he could remember of the ritual, and said, "Okay, this is something like the priest said: Dick Kaylen, I absolve you from your sin of killing ... what was his name?"

"Gordon, Gordon Wiedemeyer."

"Dick Kaylen, my friend, I absolve you from your sin of killing Gordon Wiedemeyer, in the name of the Father, and of the Son, and of the Holy Spirit. That, I believe is straight from God to you, Dick. Now your response, if you really believe and accept what I said, is 'Amen.' "

Jerry looked in his rear view mirror, and expected Kathy was praying. He hadn't thought of her praying, but in that moment he now believed without a doubt she and Patti were praying for their husbands. He prayed and waited, and then in the dark Dick uttered one quiet word, but the happiest he had ever spoken to Jerry, "Amen." And Jerry echoed his friend, "AMEN."

* * *

Friends, we all have done things, intentionally and unintentionally, which have hurt others and haunted us. Yet none of us needs go unforgiven. Please bow in prayer and hold before God that for which you need to be forgiven.

Now in the name of Jesus Christ I absolve you of your sins, in the name of the Father and of the Son and of the Holy Spirit. Amen. If you believe and accept this forgiveness, please say, "Amen."

Discussion Questions

Text: John 20:23

1. What are your immediate responses to the story?

2. If you could have a conversation with one of the characters in this story which would you speak with and what would you ask or say?

3. Do you identify with any character in the story?

4. Have the consequences of an accident haunted you?

5. Was your early religious training helpful or hurtful to you? In what ways?

6. To whom do you talk about your faith? About your painful experiences? About your deepest joys?

7. When or with whom do you confess your sins?

8. Have you left a denomination or a religion? What of the religion you left still has value for you?

9. In that Christ rewrites our lives, what from this story would you like to have happen in your life?

Text: Romans 12:14-21

Chapter 8

The Cathedral Corner Cafe

Letty looked around the cafe. The usual were present: the man who wore a plastic grocery sack on his head when it rained, and Harry who, every day, had one pant leg tucked in a boot, and one pant leg over a boot. The fellow who either cursed the wall or laughed half the time was at his table. It was hard to decide which was better: when he took his medication or when he didn't. The tall, skinny man was in the corner booth. He twitched constantly and coughed like a machine gun. Bessie was sitting on a stool at the counter. She was so large no one could sit on the stools next to her.

Without looking at her watch Letty knew it was past 8:15 a.m. because a couple dirty men came in. The grocery stores didn't receive returnable cans and bottles until 8 a.m. Letty looked over the customers as she dashed from tables to the counter, then to the kitchen and back. She saw laborers, professionals, clerks, and secretaries. She had learned the regulars and she could figure out the others. She knew the ones who would probably tip well, and she knew the couples who were not married, because the man was fawning over the woman — or over her children. She knew the men who would flirt with her. She brought the coffee pot towards the first person at the counter and he waved his hand over the cup. "All coffeed out?" she asked. He nodded. She continued down the counter, refilling cups.

Letty had worked summers at the Cathedral Corner Cafe. Then at Christmas of her junior year she quit college, came home, and became a permanent employee. But her work as a waitress took on a different tone. Now when she served a customer she said, "God bless you and your meal." A few people snorted or laughed nervously when she said it, but no one expressed resistance until Carl. He was a few years older than Letty and they had known one another in high school. He was thin and medium height; he had never left the town of Burton. If he was not moving about, almost bouncing from place to place, he was chewing his fingernails or drumming them on something. Letty walked up to the counter the first time he ordered from her, set his Number Two Special in front of him, and said, "God bless you and your meal."

"Don't say that to me," Carl said.

Letty was too surprised to respond, simply continued to serve him as she did all others. Yet still, after that first meal Carl could tell that when she put down his plate she paused as though she were saying those words silently, and he would frown.

One morning there was a party in the cafe. A secretary from the office across the street was moving away. The frosting on top of the cake spelled out, "YOU ARE FINALLY GETTING OUT OF HERE." Carl watched and listened to the chatty group. "Letty, why don't you get out of this dump?"

"You calling this cafe a dump?"

"It's a dump, and you know it. The roof leaks, the toilets back up, you shiver in the winter and sweat in the summer. The lighting is terrible — like trying to eat in a cave. If that doesn't depress you, the cowboy music will."

"You keep coming here."

"But if there was a cheaper place, closer to home I wouldn't."

"The Checkerboard Restaurant is closer to your house and they charge the same as we do."

"Letty, this is a dead-end cafe in a dead-end town. Count the empty buildings on Main Street. This town is as exciting as watching paint dry. Half the morons in the county come here between breakfast and lunch every day. You're too smart to work here. Waitresses never stay here. A couple years and they're all gone and another crop is hired to be worn out."

"I'll grant you a lot of people here treat me like a tool, or toy, and a lot of guys hit on me. I've been other places. People aren't much different anywhere. And if there really is another place better, why shouldn't I be here anyway?"

"Letty, have you ever heard that religion is the opiate of the people? That's what's happened to you. The stuff has clogged your head. Your religion is keeping you from developing as a person. This cafe is for losers."

Letty was opening her mouth to answer, but Carl got off the stool, placed two dollars and fifty cents on the counter, and left.

All day Letty pondered what Carl said. She was still thinking about Carl when she and Doris, the other waitress, met outside the Cathedral Corner Cafe the next morning at 4:45 a.m. The cook always arrived at the last minute, and he had the key. Seventy-five years ago the Roman Catholic Cathedral stood on the corner, but when it burned, the bishop found the fire to be a graceful way out of an embarrassment. Burton had not become the center of the region. Not only did the farm lands 200 miles west fill up with suburbs, but Burton and the area around it declined in population. So the burned cathedral was a way that the church headquarters could move elsewhere. Ever since the fire the corner was called "Cathedral Corner" though fewer and fewer citizens knew why.

Letty was aware when Carl came in that morning, but she was not about to start a conversation about God. Carl was ready to debate at the drop of a hat. He was like a bomb she knew would go off sometime. Three weeks later Letty brought a meal to a person sitting at the counter next to Carl. She said, "God bless you and your meal."

Carl opened up on her, "Letty, this is not normal. This is not the usual thing you hear waitresses say. People don't ask you for this blessing thing. You ought to cut it out. You didn't used to do it. What's the matter with you?"

Letty had thought carefully about what she would say. "You're right. But at college I became a Christian. It wasn't usual for me to say such things before. I didn't plan to say it now. I came back to work that first day and picked up an order. Rollie was at the counter waiting for his corned beef hash with extra green peppers. I put his plate down in front of him and the words just came out, 'God bless you and your meal.' Rollie was surprised, but he looked up at me with this big smile, and said, 'Thank you, daughter.' I've said it ever since because that's who I am and what I want for everyone. I'm not trying to pry anyone into faith. I just believe God is here and God wants me to bless these people for him."

Carl stood up abruptly. "The eggs taste like Styrofoam. Put it on my tab." He walked quickly towards the door speaking over his shoulder, "Letty, who do you think you are, Mother Teresa?"

Carl spent the rest of the week eating breakfasts on the other side of the cafe, Doris' side, even though he could not smoke there. But nine days later he walked in and came right up to the counter. "Morning, Carl," Letty said. "The usual?"

"Yeah, Letty. But first. What I said last week. I'm sorry. I've been bothered lately."

"Oh?"

"My dad is dying in Mississippi. I think about it all the time."

"I remember your dad. He worked for the railroad."

"Yeah. Always did. If he lives till next week I'll see him before he dies. That's as soon as I can get off work."

"I'm sorry, Carl. I'll remember him in my ..." Letty stopped, but Carl said, "You might as well. The doctors say there's nothing they can do. But I'd like to talk with him before he dies."

Carl did not return to the cafe for half a month. Letty thought about him every day. When he did return he was waiting when the cook raised the shade at six, turned over the "Open" sign in the window, and unlocked the door. Carl was smoking when he walked in and lit another cigarette before Letty came with the coffee. He was the only customer at the counter, his shoulders sloped toward his thin chest. Before Letty spoke, Carl said, "Dad died."

"I thought that's where you were. Did you get to see him?"

"Yeah. I was there three days before he died."

"How did it go?"

"He was conscious for a couple days, but nothing was good about it. Everything and everyone was wrong. And I don't know why. And I can't fix it."

"Did you talk a lot?"

"Some, but he never did understand me, and I know I never understood him. All he talked about was how we four kids should split the life insurance, and divide up the stuff in his double-wide. No matter how I tried to get around to what has been between us for years he wouldn't talk seriously. I wanted to tell him what I'd

70

been thinking about. I wanted to tell him what you said about your life changing." Carl drummed his fingers on the counter.

"You loved your dad." Her tone was between a statement and a question.

"I don't know. In some ways he was a really nice guy. Everybody liked him. He tried to be a good father. I guess it's just that he didn't love me the way I wanted. I suppose I didn't love him the way he wanted either."

Carl looked silently out the window. "I didn't know how to get around to talking about what's important. I was trying, but it didn't work. I lost again."

Carl hung his head. Letty poured a cup of coffee and slid it between his hands. She waited, but he said nothing more. Finally she asked, "Carl, would you like my usual?"

He stared at her for a full three seconds, then as he looked down he spoke just loud enough for her to hear, "Yeah. Yeah, I think I need your usual real bad."

He hung his head, and clasped his hands around his coffee cup. As Letty had never done before, she reached across the counter and put her hand on his shoulder. She bowed her head, and whispered, "God, bless Carl and the memories of his father."

Then as though she had just done the most natural thing in the world, Letty was off to the kitchen to place Carl's order for the Cathedral Corner Cafe's Number Two Special.

* * *

Receive the blessing: May God Almighty, Father of our Lord Jesus Christ, giver of the Holy Spirit, bless you where you eat and where you work, where you suffer and where you serve, now and forever. Amen.

Discussion Questions

Text: Romans 12:14-21

1. What are your immediate responses to the story?

2. If you could have a conversation with one of the characters in this story, which would you speak with and what would you ask or say?

3. Do you identify with any character in the story?

4. Have you told a non-Christian about your faith in Christ?

5. Have you experienced rejection because of your faith?

6. Have you blessed someone, or been blessed by someone? What were the circumstances? What was it like?

7. If someone asked you, "Where and how do you serve Christ," what would you answer?

8. In that Christ rewrites our lives, what from this story would you like to have happen in your life?

Chapter 9

Why Do *People Suffer?*

Susan Ingraham was late for worship, but no one could tell she was hurrying — regular, sharp gait, everything about her seemed shiny and healthy. At 34 Miss Ingraham was startlingly beautiful, especially to twelve year old Chrissy Dillenburger. Chrissy was captivated by her since the day Susan came to worship wearing a plain black dress, black shoes, perfect lipstick and a gold brooch. First thing in the car going home Chrissy said, "Did you see Miss Ingraham? That dress — and the lipstick was just right for her outfit!"

Unknown to Susan, Chrissy waited for her every Sunday, and so today, instead of listening to the Scripture reading, Chrissy was glancing backwards as the regal Miss Ingraham brushed past the usher, politely received a bulletin, and sat in the next to the last pew. Susan wore a dark brown tweed suit with a gold silk kerchief around her neck. For Chrissy, worship could begin.

"As I announced, the sermon this morning is about why people suffer. Our Christian era plus the centuries of our Jewish ancestors, add up to four thousand years to reflect upon the problem, and various answers are given. The first answer is that in this world people get what they deserve. Of course the suffering might not be exactly in proportion to our sins or crimes, but basically our deeds catch up with us, either as an individual or as a species. God has planned life to operate this way, and thus suffering is God's judgment upon us."

Susan Ingraham, registered nurse and licensed midwife, sat comfortably straight in her pew, as though she had been taught how to sit in model's school. Her perfectly formed half smile was so pleasant it warmed all who saw her — especially Chrissy. In Susan's mind she shrieked, "You can't hold a dying infant in your hands trying with all your wit and might to blow and pump life into it while its mother groans in hemorrhage beside you — you can't do that and offer this casual, thin, brittle reason for why such a thing would happen. Of course we must take the consequences of our actions, and our actions lap over onto our children, but you are accusing God of killing a child because of what the parents did. No court would uphold allowing anyone to kill the child for the sin of the parent or society. You are saying God is less moral than our most basic laws."

Seldom did Susan notice the reader board outside the church building; in fact the church was not on her usual route from home to work. But this week she passed the church as she drove from the hospital to the police station and there in white letters behind glass was the sermon title: "Why People Suffer." The sermon title followed her all week like a wounded bear trying to take vengeance upon its hunter. She was so upset she considered that for the sake of others she should not attend worship. Early Sunday morning she paced around her apartment; then at almost 11 a.m., with one lunge, she was out the door and running to her car. She came to worship with a pocket full of ugly questions and she was ready to do serious battle.

"Another explanation for human suffering is that God has reasons we will never understand. God's ways are beyond ours, not only in quantity, but also in quality. Thus God sees the large picture, we see only a few shards of color."

"Sure," Susan thought, "Adolf Hitler had reasons we could never understand. But the Bible continually tells us God is merciful and forgiving. God gave us Jesus and Jesus didn't go around killing people. That's hard data. What kind of ruined mind would say God has reasons for allowing people to die when Jesus spent his whole career healing and helping? Don't theologians take a course in logic? If God has reasons for allowing people to suffer, how come Jesus was absolutely opposed to suffering?"

This week she had thought intently and spoken much to God about suffering. Susan was the most careful of the careful. She was a nurse mid-wife and owned the business with three other mid-wives which delivered more children by midwifery per capita than was done by any other business in any other city in the United States. Although she promised not to tell, a doctor had even consulted with her once.

Adding all her life's miseries together, this week's tragedies outweighed them all. She had grabbed dead babies from the birth canal before, and babies had died soon after her assist into life — but nothing like this child's death or what followed. The delivery had been strange from the start. No indication on the monitors, no numbers on read-outs or lines on graphs told toward doom. Something was wrong beyond mechanical sensing. When the mother finally dilated ten centimeters Susan again slipped her fingers up the birth canal and realized the child was face up. The mother pushed and pushed. Hours went by. Just sweat, pain, tears. No progress.

It was after the surgery team was called to do a Caesarean delivery that Susan again placed her hand on the child's head and she was swept with a sense that the child would not live. No reason. Nothing scientific. The moment she sensed the baby was going to die Susan felt a sensation from her right hand snap up her arm and hit her entire body with a thud. There was nothing she could do or say. There were no indications of anything life-threatening to child or mother. But the child died within an hour after birth — no matter the heroic work of two pediatricians. The second tragedy smashed into Susan the next day, when Carrie, the mother of the dead new-born, committed suicide.

"There are certainly problems with any thinking about why we suffer, but a further reason is that suffering builds our character. When everything in life is skating along smoothly, we do not gain strong muscles or sharp reflexes. Suffering is the spiritual resistance against which God has decided we individuals need to grow strong and which corporately ennobles us as a race."

Susan parried, "Am I to repeat this to suffering folk? Am I to spill such a weak ointment onto a wound and call it medicine? Can I tell that to Carrie's mother who is now bereft of her long-loved child, and of her expected grandchild? All this for a lesson? What are we supposed to learn? This is to make me better? At least Carrie's mother had a sad, polite policeman knock at her door to inform her. Does it build more character for me to sit alone with a cup of coffee and hear it on the radio?"

Susan had come to know and love Carrie and her mother Hazel. The three of them, over the months of the pregnancy, not only planned for the birth, but through their conversations Carrie, unwed at 19, decided to keep the child instead of giving it up for adoption. Susan and Hazel were satisfied that Carrie had made the right decision and that the child would have a good home.

Susan sat in worship counting her failures and calculating the pain of all involved. "How many dead teenagers have to be pulled from prom-night wrecks? How many boats have to sink with all hands lost or planes crash with all passengers killed? How many wars need to be fought before we have enough character? You'd think God would have some better way to build our character."

"The church also teaches that in heaven God will compensate us for all the partial justice done in this world. We can't see it here, but God will execute perfect justice in heaven. In heaven the loss we have experienced will be compensated; the suffering we have endured will be repaid."

Not a muscle on Susan's face moved, but she felt heavy. "Do we really need to make excuses for God? Must we justify God in all this and say God's not to blame? Or are we copying insurance companies' blasphemies, naming all that we can't control 'Acts of God'? Do we have to relate absolutely everything that happens to God? Jesus didn't blame God. He set out to attack Satan and the demons. Need we besmirch God's reputation in every discussion of tidal waves, wars, epidemics, hurricanes, accidents, and crimes? But if God is somehow bound up with everything in this life, how do we think about suffering and how can we tug some vital, wiggling meaning into this air we breathe?"

"It is important to note that although there is truth in all the reasons that people offer for our suffering, and Scripture points to these and other reasons, none of them alone and not all of them together answer enough questions. There is one focus for Christians concerning suffering. Our text this morning is Jesus on the cross, and his last words in the Gospel of Mark are, 'My God, my God, why have you forsaken me?' As Christians, this is where we both start and end our reasoning about human suffering: at Jesus' cross. The Bible does not say that God makes Jesus suffer, but since God is in Jesus, we know that God suffers with us. In Jesus' cross God offers us something beyond our questions, God gives us a person to suffer with us and for us.

"When we have pulled every answer from the centuries of Christian thought, when we have offered every consolation that for millennia people have spoken to those who suffer, we end with our Lord Jesus on the cross, whose question about why he suffered was not immediately answered. It would be satisfying if we had more answers, but the fact of our Christian faith over the centuries demonstrates that Jesus' suffering for us and with us is enough — maybe not enough to answer all our questions, but enough to help us live faithfully. For all of humanity's billions of bitter tears and wasted suffering, God did not waste any of Jesus' tears or suffering, but used them to love us.

"If you cry out to the universe, 'My God, my God, why have you forsaken me?' you take your place next to Jesus. It might not be a comfortable place. You might even feel as though you are being crucified, but you are beside the one person who loves you through everything: joy and suffering, certainty and doubt, life and death. In the end we cannot answer why people suffer; but we commend to all the God who suffered for us and with us in Jesus the Christ."

At the benediction Susan left immediately. Chrissy was after her, if only to view her leaving. Chrissy gained a final glimpse of dark brown tweed as Susan glided down the last of the church steps and briskly walked around the corner. The glance was worth it. To Chrissy Susan seemed everything a Christian woman should be.

Discussion Questions

Text: Mark 15:33-39

1.   What are your immediate reactions to the story?

2. If you could have a conversation with one of the characters in this story, which would you speak with and what would you ask or say?

3. Do you identify with any character in the story?

4. Name some of the poor or sub-Christian reasons you have heard about why people suffer.

5. Which of the reasons given for human suffering makes the most sense to you?

6. How are your experiences, feelings, and thoughts about suffering the same as Susan's and different from Susan's?

7. Have you struggled to understand God's part in a specific instance of human suffering?

8. In that Christ rewrites our lives, what from this story would you like to have happen in your life?

Text: John 11:25-26

Chapter 10

The L & L Ranch

Being a woman causes difficulties in being a pastor, not only because many men think I should not be a pastor, but some women also. I suffer from loneliness for women colleagues — especially in a small town, a pioneer where I did not want to be a pioneer. Yet I am called to be a pastor and the blessings far outweigh the difficulties: the blessings of ministering to those who are coming to birth in faith, the blessing of standing at the Lord's table offering grace that can be tasted, the blessing of sharing with people who honestly question their faith and themselves.

I spent 23 years as a member of a large, active church. I was confirmed there both in my faith and in my gifts for ministry. The fall after our second child graduated from college — which was six and a half years after my husband, Dean, died — I went to seminary for three splendid years of theological study. My first call as pastor came three and a half years ago to this small congregation in the village of Anchorton. The congregation had never had a female pastor before, and I think they called me because no one else would come; so the congregation now has a middle-aged female as pastor and not all parishioners are pleased with me or my approach to faith.

In my first two years here I tried too hard to reach them in my calling, teaching, and organizing ministry. In my sermons I struggled to arrive at a common understanding with them. No preacher set out more self-consciously to communicate with a congregation. I tried preaching like Fred Craddock, Paul Tillich, then Peter Marshall, and finally Barbara Brown Taylor. None of these styles fit me, and none seemed to reach the congregation. In fact, little of what I have tried has gotten me into the door of the congregation's heart. I remain the outsider.

Even calling at the hospital is strange for me. One day as I drove into the hospital parking lot, I saw the Roman Catholic priest — whom the Catholics share with the communities of Aiken and Fivecorners. As he drove by I saw his black coat and bright white collar. No problem identifying him as a priest. The male Protestant clergy seem to have no difficulties of identity either, partly because they carry four pound Bibles to the hospital. But I was going to visit a man I hardly knew. I was the first pastor to visit him wearing a skirt, though it was below the knee and tan. I wore a blue blazer, and a blouse with a bow, which I hoped would appear something like a necktie.

As I walked nervously to Leo Swelton's room I pondered again the differences between men and women. If I were a man calling on a man I could probably say something about the jobs we had, the sports we liked, maybe hunting or fishing, even make some sideways joke about sex. It is so much easier for me to call on women. We talk about our children, decorating our homes, or about our flowers or plants. I mention my quilting. We share recipes. Sometimes we even complain about men. And thus I more easily speak with women about faith.

I peeked tentatively into room 116 and saw Leo Swelton upon his bed, eyes closed. He was a small person, shorter than I, and there are not many men around shorter than my five feet three inches. I walked in quietly, and was about to offer a silent prayer over him, when he opened his eyes. We spoke almost at the same time, "Hello." Then I stood, not knowing what next to say, while he lay in the bed wondering, I thought, if I would ever speak again.

But obviously, that was not what he was thinking. In almost a whisper he said, "I have a question for you."

"Yes."

"How are Christians supposed to die?"

I was startled at his bluntness, but I knew exactly how to respond. I restated his question, "You are wondering how Christians are supposed to die." I had learned in counseling to reflect people's feelings and thoughts. It helps them continue to talk and work out their own problems — it also saves the counselor from answering questions.

"Yes," he said clearly, "I want to know how Christians are supposed to die."

I had reflected this idea once, so I did not know what to say. I asked, "What do you mean?"

He spoke a little louder, "Is there a way Christians are supposed to die?"

I took a couple of shallow breaths and, not knowing what else to do, I answered, "Christians die as they live — by faith in God's grace through Christ. If you want to know if there is a correct way to die, I think the Bible makes it clear that as we don't impress God by living a perfect life, so we don't impress God by dying a perfect death. In life or death, we rely upon God's grace and forgiveness."

Leo Swelton stared into my eyes, but said nothing more. I do not think I said what he expected, and maybe not what he needed. I could tell he was tired, and after a few chatty exchanges I left, but I walked down the hospital hallway and out to my car wondering: Could not God overcome the difficulties of male to female communication by granting a male and female pastor to each gathering of Christians?

The next day visiting Leo I found something we could share: his grandchildren were about the age of my children. So we passed three or four minutes conversing about our progeny, yet I did not have the courage to ask him about Lilly.

Mr. and Mrs. Nekte had informed me about Leo and his wife, Lilly. Mr. and Mrs. Nekte (and clearly they wanted me to call them Mr. and Mrs.) were a couple in the congregation who committed mutual, serial, self-inflicted suffering. They were each convinced that life had treated them badly and that everyone they met was called upon to compensate for their deficiencies — those things that they had never been given, or that life had stolen from them. Mr. Nekte called me "Jill," Mrs. Nekte called me "Pastor Wharing." Every Sunday I threw large chunks of the good news of God's grace in their direction; but their actions every Monday proved that I either threw it wrongly, or they dropped it when it got to them, because grace did not seem to affect them.

It was Mr. Nekte, in his usual way, who apprised me that Leo was ill. At the door after worship he said, "Have you seen Leo

Swelton in the hospital?" He had spoken about Leo and Lilly before and usually he would say, "Leo and his little wife," or "Lilly and her little husband." His question sounded like an accusation: "Are you doing your job?" When I answered, "I didn't know he was in the hospital," he honed the edges upon his words, "You better get up to see him, he's dying." I considered asserting that I did not take mind-reading in college and it would help if people would tell me things instead of assuming that I know, or demanding that I know, but I only said, "Mmmm."

Although the Nektes were determined to punish all the world for its gross unfairness to them, yet even Mrs. Nekte had only a few barbs in her voice when she mentioned Lilly. One evening at a potluck she told me the chapter of the Sweltons in the community's history. Early in my ministry it became clear that she appointed herself the congregation's official historian for each new pastor. She informed me about church members, especially those deceased or who had quit the church. Also she disclosed the county's earliest history. I considered her talks as, "The world according to Mrs. Nekte."

That evening she began by describing the various crops of the county and which ones had been planted first and where. When she got to the L & L Ranch, she said, "Lilly named it the L & L Ranch, you know, though it was a farm and not a ranch, and farms in these parts don't have names. I probably heard Lilly tell it a dozen times. She'd mention to someone the name of the farm and they'd ask, 'Does the L & L stand for Leo and Lilly?' She'd answer, 'Well, if you ask Leo, it stands for Leo and Lilly, but if you ask me, it stands for Lilly and Leo.' Yet, and this comes from knowing someone over four decades, about the time her kids left home, her story changed so that Leo would say it was Lilly and Leo's, and Lilly that it was Leo and Lilly's. If she really wanted to confuse someone — I heard her at a wedding reception talking with guests from New York City — she said she didn't name the L & L Ranch for people, but for the centennial. When they asked, 'What centennial?' She said, 'Of 1840.' Then she laughed, her little elf face so small that as you looked at her from the front, you almost couldn't see her chin until her mouth was open.

"Lilly was always laughing, often at the jokes she made herself. We [I assumed Mr. Nekte and herself] always said that Lilly was not just Leo's wife, she was his private entertainer. When Lilly died, we all expected Leo to die soon."

I reviewed Mrs. Nekte's rendition of Lilly and Leo's relationship as I went to visit Leo again the next day.

Leo was weak and moved little while I was with him. I figured it was gracious of me to speak first and save him the effort. "I know you're tired, Leo. I wanted you to know I've been praying for you."

He closed his eyes as he nodded his head slightly, thanking me. Since we had talked about our children and grandchildren I feared that we had exhausted our commonalities. Then he squarely focused upon my eyes as if he wanted to talk, and as if what he had to say was important. But we both remained silent. Finally I said, "I never met Lilly. I wish I had. People tell me she was quite a joker."

As though mention of Lilly gave Leo energy he rolled his head a little more in my direction and said, "She was a dear."

I asked, "How long has she been dead?"

"Nine years last May. She went suddenly, just when we were ready to enjoy our retirement." It was hard for Leo to speak, but he continued, "In less than a week she slid from healthy to bedridden. The doctors agreed a heart valve needed repair. Well, it was fixed but after that a string of strokes. Within two and a half months she was gone."

Leo fell silent, again staring at me. I waited. Finally he closed his eyes getting ready to speak. He spoke with his eyes shut. "You're a widow," he said.

"Yes. Dean has been dead eleven years, eleven years last November. Bard was in junior high and Joanne was in grade school."

Again he closed his eyes and asked me, with his eyes shut, "Did he die suddenly?" Then he opened his eyes to see and hear my answer.

"We had about six months to prepare for his death."

"Did he die well?"

His words struck me like a Cadillac at 75 miles an hour. First thing I knew tears flowed down my face, mascara splattered my blouse. Happens every time I am happy or sad, angry or confused. I cry. I thought I had finished my crying for Dean, thought it was over years ago, enough tears to flush the eyes of everyone in the county. But I cried because I missed Dean every day and wished we were sharing life together now that I was a pastor. And I cried because Leo, despite his pain and loss, asked about mine. Leo's concern for me, even in his suffering, toppled me over into ministry. At that moment I was certainly thinking about myself, yet I was more concerned about Leo. My tears told me this.

I have a friend who tells me every time we meet that the newest book, conversation, seminar, or movie "has changed my life." I suspect television commercials will next be added to her list. Not me. I change slowly. But standing with Leo I was finishing some changing that had slowly occurred within me.

Did he die well, this man who put four teaspoons of sugar in his coffee and rattled the spoon in his cup until he drank it all? Did he die well, this man who wore his faded grey high school baseball cap when he mowed the lawn? Said he would wear it the rest of his life, and he did. It hangs now in Bard's garage. Did he die well, this man whom I still miss seeing sitting on the toilet when I get out of the shower, this man whom I remember on every Christmas Eve with the kids beside him as he read them Dickens' *A Christmas Carol?*

Did he die well? He yelled, wept, mumbled, prayed. We talked for hours, trying to get everything in the world said before he died. We planned the rest of my life, and then we just sat in silence looking at one another. Did he die well?

I spoke quietly, "Yes, and Lilly?"

"Yes," Leo said.

I did not wipe my face; that would have been for my sake. With my nose and eyes dripping all over my blazer I simply reached for Leo's hands and he for mine. I held Leo's hands for his sake. And once more I choked out, "Yes," for both of us, and nodded my head.

Leo coughed, giving me a chance to move slightly, and he slowly released my hands. He was exhausted. I pulled a chair near, sat down, put one hand on his and said, "I'll stay until you sleep."

For the next two days, Leo reached for my hands as soon as I stepped in the room. On the third day he was ready to speak, as if he had saved his strength for my coming. "Was a time," he spoke weakly, "I wasn't sure a woman could be a pastor."

"Was a time," I said, "I wasn't sure a lot of men could be Christians."

He looked confused, but he held my hands tightly, with no energy left to speak. He did not have to say anything for my sake, and probably not for his either. Every day when I visited I prayed for him, and as long as he knew me we held hands, all four hands.

His funeral was on a Saturday and when friends stood to speak about Leo they spoke of both Lilly and Leo, as though until Leo died they could not speak freely about Lilly, and perhaps until Leo died they could not fully grieve for Lilly, because Leo and Lilly came so close to living one life.

I cannot say that Leo changed me. There is nothing I believe afterwards that I did not believe before Leo's death; although I suppose I believe it deeper. No, I have not been changed much in my beliefs. I still believe that we do not live nor die perfectly; and I know that I did not minister perfectly to Leo in his living or his dying.

Since there is not a lot for a single, middle-aged, female pastor to do in this small rural town I have taken to driving in the country. I have found the old L & L Ranch. I see the farm trucks, pickup, car, tractors, and bicycles. Sitting for a moment in my car on the county road I wonder about the grace of God that operated here. I pray that it is as real for those who now own this farm. Because here, between the house, barn, and outbuildings, between where Leo and Lilly lived and where they worked and where they worshiped, Christ walked with them, teaching them how to live, and by doing so, teaching them enough about how to die.

* * *

85

John, chapter 11, verses 25 and 26: "Jesus said to her, 'I am the resurrection and the life. Those who believe in me, even though they die, will live, and everyone who lives and believes in me will never die. Do you believe this?' "

Let us pray: Our loving God, you have been among us in our Lord Jesus. Through him you granted us eternal life that begins now and never stops. Help us to trust him, by how we live, what we say, whom we love, and how we die. We have no other hope in life or death. In his name we pray. Amen.

Discussion Questions

Text: John 11:25-26

1. What immediate responses do you have to the story?

2. If you could have a conversation with one of the characters in this story which would you speak with and what would you ask or say?

3. Do you identify with any character in the story?

4. Have you felt like an outsider? In a community? In a church?

5. Has someone reached out to you, even through his or her own pain?

6. How has your relationship with a dying person affected your life and faith?

7. In that Christ rewrites our lives, what from this story would you like to have happen in your life?

Text: Galatians 5:22-23

Chapter 11

What Really Matters

Larry and Evelyn Schmidt lay awake long past their usual time for sleep. It was midnight at least. They awaited a telephone call from their son-in-law Jeff. Their daughter Annie was in labor, and at ten o'clock they finally went to bed, but without hope of sleeping. Larry and Evelyn had been married 42 years, and only now awaited the birth of their first grandchild. All evening they'd been in the mood to talk, recounting Larry Junior's birth, eleven years after their marriage, and then the surprise of Annie, eight years later.

Larry Junior was always "Little Larry" until his sophomore year in high school when he was taller than his father and declared he was no longer "Little Larry." It took all involved — friends and relatives — a few years to get used to, but especially when Larry starred in basketball, and went on to play his first two years of college, the word "Little" was doomed. Larry Junior was determined to be a teacher and a basketball coach. When someone argued that he could earn much more money in other professions, Larry Junior said, "Being a teacher and coach is enough for me."

Larry and Evelyn had always wanted children; then when Larry Junior was born they wanted more children, and with what medical help was available they attempted to do so. They had the disappointment, however, of three miscarriages. Finally, when Evelyn was 40 and Larry 41 they paid a surgeon to make sure that "contra-" would be placed permanently before "-ception." Only then did Evelyn become pregnant with their miracle child.

That evening after Jeff had phoned to say that Annie's contractions were five minutes apart and they were leaving for the hospital, Larry and Evelyn had talked about the mystery and joy of their first child Larry Junior. Larry said, "He pretty well raised us."

"He certainly taught us how to be parents," Evelyn said.

Larry Junior would always be their mystery child — the child who introduced them to the mysterious love that grows in those who nurture children. But then Annie came along when Larry was eight, and she was always the miracle child. Two very special children. They had wanted more, but they had enough.

Yet even with a miracle in the house, life began a slow decline for Larry and Evelyn. Evelyn went through a difficult early menopause, and suffered physically and emotionally for years, consulting many physicians and counselors. Larry had his own crises. He could say honestly he had never committed adultery, but adding up all his flirtings they did not come much short of adultery. And then Annie was diagnosed with polio. Not supposed to happen. One in a million chance. They never knew if it was because of an ineffective batch of vaccine, or if the vaccine itself gave the disease. But Annie at seven was stricken. The effects of the disease hit the whole household. Larry and Evelyn naturally turned their attention to Annie, and did their best to parent Larry Junior, but they knew he did not get all the love he needed. Yet he had his sports and friends, and he always managed to survive.

For Annie the virus meant weeks in the hospital and then months of convalescence, and Evelyn and Larry learned how to manipulate her body to keep her muscles supple. But emotionally it was more than Larry could do. He tried a few times, but emotionally he was unable to cause Annie pain. So while Annie was recovering, not only did Evelyn begin home schooling, but three times a day Evelyn lifted Annie into a hot bath and pressed and twisted and manipulated her body until Annie's own commands to her left leg would work again. Each treatment was a dose of hell. Annie would cry; Evelyn would cry. And when Larry was home, he would stand outside the bathroom and cry.

One evening while Larry was standing hopeless and helpless outside the bathroom door — Annie begging to stop and Evelyn encouraging Annie for a couple more repetitions — Larry decided he had no more resources. He was out, dry, depleted, empty. He simply could not go on and did not have the slightest idea how he had managed until now. Years had passed since he told Evelyn how miserable he was, and both of them had shriveled emotionally under the burden of Annie's illness. But standing there Larry decided to go to church on Sunday, and he promised whoever might be above that he would do so. On Sunday, Larry merely announced to Evelyn he was going to church, and left. They had a church to attend on Easter and Christmas Eve, so he knew the way there, and knew the pastor's name, even though they had never spoken beyond a handshake at the door.

This morning, Larry did not see the pastor. When it was a time for the sermon, a woman stood up behind the pulpit and apologized that Pastor Darrell was on vacation and she was giving the sermon. Larry's heart sank. Of all the days to get stuck with a substitute. But he was desperate enough to listen. The lady in the pulpit said, "There is a lot I don't know or understand about the Bible, about the New Testament, about Paul, about his Galatian letter, but you can't live by what you don't understand. You have to live by what you believe. So out of all the Bible, I chose Galatians 5:22-23 to talk about. Because Jesus has been raised from the dead, he sends his Holy Spirit to produce in us the same kind of life he lived, which is a life filled with love, joy, peace, patience, kindness, goodness, faithfulness, gentleness, and self-control. The main reason I believe in Jesus' resurrection is that I believe the Holy Spirit works in my life to bring about this character of Jesus — what Paul named, 'the fruit of the Spirit.' "

That afternoon Larry asked Little Larry — (Sorry, Larry Junior) — to please use his calligraphy pen and write the contents of Galatians 5:22-23. The next day Larry had the paper framed and he hung it in the bedroom over the head of his and Evie's bed. And the next Sunday Larry went to church again, telling Evie she could come along if she wanted, but he was going. He had heard all the excuses for not going to church, the hypocrites, the asking for money; but he went to church that Sunday and the next Sunday. Then Evie started to attend with him, and when Annie was able they brought the kids. And the whole family was soon in Sunday school classes, and youth groups, and adult groups, as the family formed itself around the resurrected Jesus and into his body, the church.

Annie recovered but with a limp. Even with one shoe built up, she limped, always would; but she more than limped, she skipped. The little kid was so glad to be out of the house and back to school that as her strength slowly returned so did her skip. People on the street would see her going to school and note the skip and talk to one another about it. The Schmidts' neighbor, Lila Sontag, told her son and his wife when they visited her. The next morning at 7:35 the three of them were at the window to watch Annie skip to school. Lila said, "See what I mean?"

Her son answered, "Yeah, a skip with a hitch. Seems like the happiest kid on the block."

Larry Junior went to the university and became a teacher and coach, and was pretty good at both; but a couple of years into the teaching profession, he phoned his parents and said, "I think God is calling me to be a pastor. What do you think?"

They were both positive about the idea, but he seemed to want them to say more. "Son," Larry said, "I don't know a lot about the Bible or the Christian faith — a lot I don't know about Jesus and Paul and the rest of them. But you can't live by what you don't understand. You've got to live by what you believe. I believe that Jesus was raised from the dead and that his Holy Spirit is here to help us live as he did. I feel God's Spirit with me every day, trying to make me more like the character of Jesus. I think God's Spirit has got hold of you too."

Larry Junior attended seminary, met his wife there, graduated, was ordained, and now was serving his second congregation. His son's sermons usually disappointed Larry Senior. "They all sound like classroom lectures," often so dull Larry Senior would nod off. But Larry Junior's congregations grew and his parishioners loved him. Many things mattered far more than how he preached.

Years later Annie followed her brother's footsteps, though of course they did not match exactly, to the University and a teaching degree. She met Jeff there and brought him home to meet the folks. But as Larry said, "Jeff is one of the three quietest people I've ever met and I can't remember the other two."

Evie suggested, "Maybe if we'd just grab him by the neck and shake him he'd talk to us." They could hardly get more than "Yes" or "No." But how he loved Annie, and when he and Annie were alone they chattered like chipmunks.

They married immediately after college and set off to be teachers in a small town 300 miles east of Larry and Evie. For all the time it took Larry and Evie to get pregnant, the opposite occurred with Jeff and Annie. For Annie it became a race to see which would come first, the end of her first year of teaching or her baby.

So Larry and Evie Schmidt lay awake and awaited the phone call. Together they had reviewed their children's births — the mystery and the miracle of physical life through them to others. Now they prayed for the life soon to enter the world through Annie. Maybe they had been to sleep, hard to tell; but around two the phone rang. Each leaped from bed. Larry got to the phone first. It was Jeff, "Dad, this is Jeff."

"Yes, Jeff, how's it going?"

"Mother and infant doing well."

"That's wonderful," Larry said.

"I'm going to phone Larry Junior now and get back to Annie."

"Thank you, Jeff." He hung up and turned to Evie, "Jeff said, 'Mother and infant doing well.' He certainly *is* a man of few words."

"But Lar, is it a boy or girl?"

Larry looked at her blankly, as if it were the last thing on his mind. "He didn't say."

They stood staring foolishly at one another and Larry said, "I guess it doesn't really matter."

What really mattered was what Larry believed years before, what he practiced every day, and what was printed in Larry Junior's careful handwriting on the plaque over their bed, "But the fruit of the Spirit is love, joy, peace, patience, kindness, goodness, faithfulness, gentleness, self-control; against such there is no law.

> The Apostle Paul
> Galatians Chapter Five
> Verses Twenty-Two and Twenty-Three."

Discussion Questions

Text: Galatians 5:22-23

1. What immediate responses do you have to the story?

2. If you could have a conversation with one of the characters in this story which would you speak with and what would you ask or say?

3. Do you identify with any character in the story?

4. Who has suffered most in your life — your spouse, children, parents, siblings or yourself? What did that suffering do to your relationships with these people? What did the suffering do to your relationship with God?

5. Can you name a turning point in your life or faith?

6. What caused your greatest step in Christian maturity? What was going on? Who was involved? What were the circumstances?

7. In the last half of your life (or, if you became a Christian later in life, the last half of your Christian life) what difference has Christ made in your personality or character, in your behavior or lifestyle?

8. In that Christ rewrites our lives, what from this story would you like to have happen in your life?

Text: 1 John 3:18

Chapter 12

The Half Pencil Doctor

Since his dying father placed a hand on his and asked that his ashes be taken to Bloomfield, Iowa, and while there an envelope be delivered to a Doctor Francis Casparis, Roger decided that he had better do it. His father had said, "I have metastatic cancer, and I will be dead within a week." And his father insisted that the envelope go to Iowa with his remains. His father said that Doctor Casparis had saved his life and that the doctor would tell Roger about it, and would help him also.

Roger Leeth stood helplessly by his father's hospital bed. "All I need right now," he thought, "with the divorce and custody dispute, to have a father I hardly know make demands upon me. He is as much a mystery to me dying as living."

But at least Diana allowed Roger to take along their eight-year-old son, Craig, to Iowa. Craig had slightly known his grandfather and being along to take the ashes to the cemetery might help him. Plus, Roger could deliver Craig to Diana's parents for the summer, but Roger must deliver Craig in less than a week, because that was the time provisionally allowed by the judge.

"Craig gets the same crazy arrangement as I did," Roger mumbled as he packed the car the afternoon of his father's memorial service. By 4 p.m. Roger and Craig started the three days' trip east to Iowa. For the first few hours Roger drove through rain. "What have you been studying in school lately?"

"Not much."

"How's your math?"

"Okay."

"Do you have Social Studies?"

"Yeah."

"Do you use a computer in your classroom?"

"Uh huh."

"What kind is it?"

Soon Craig slept and Roger thought about the week he had spent each summer with his father: "Each summer at the airport Father would greet me with a handshake. In his suit he looked like a sack of bones — joints stuck out through his clothes, his shoulders like an old horse. Once out of the airport, I read for a week. Nothing to do except sit silently at meals and wait for the final handshake at the airport. Father continued to work, made no difference whether I was there. He'd take me to the clinic with my book and I'd sit in the waiting room — just I and the patients and his nurse/receptionist. The waiting room was full of patients no matter how slow Father was — always moved slowly, seemed to take too long at everything. Father would appear with one patient and disappear with another.

"Occasionally, on a hot afternoon when undressing was not necessary, Father would leave the door of the exam room open and I'd see him sitting there listening. I remember him with a woman he obviously knew well. I could see him facing the open door, but from behind I could only see her shoulder. He sat for half an hour with his lips pursed. Occasionally he nodded. Then he stood, and came out to write a prescription. No 'good-bye' from him in the waiting room; but the woman smiled as if she had been healed of leprosy.

"Father placed his hand on her shoulder as they parted, as Diana used to touch me when we said good-bye. Before we were married her touch gave me goose pimples. No touching now for months. Our entire relationship overturned so that I am repulsed by the one who attracted me. She was as beautiful as a statue, a face with classical lines — more Greek than Roman. Now when I remember Diana I see her clenched teeth and tight jaw, and the sagging neck which before I never mentioned; but it pleases me greatly that her neck will be as fat as her mother's."

Three days east across the United States, Iowa was as far as Roger unfolded the map for Craig to follow. Every day trying to find things to talk about with Craig until Craig finally put on his Walkman earphones or started to play one of his three electronic games. Every day with scenes of Diana before him: gorgeous and beckoning, ugly and hateful. Every day remembering the silent summers with his father, and then the few minutes in his father's hospital room, and hourly fingering the lumpy envelope to deliver to Doctor Francis Casparis, who had saved his father's life, and who was to help him also.

The rain was vicious for the last hundred miles into Bloomfield, the windshield wipers inadequate for safe driving. But at 11 a.m. on day three of their trek, Roger and Craig, shaking the rainwater from their coats, entered the Woodward Care Center, Roger carrying an envelope. They sidestepped residents in wheelchairs, passed the physical therapy room, then beside the glassed-in dining hall to room 121. "Doctor Casparis?"

A tiny man with wispy, ashen hair sat in a wheelchair between a neatly made bed and a night stand covered with photographs and stacks of opened mail. "Doctor Casparis, my name is Roger Leeth. My father was Doctor Lester Leeth. He died last week. He asked me to bring his ashes to Bloomfield and to deliver this envelope to you." Roger held the envelope in front of the thin person in the wheelchair. The old man glanced upon the envelope less than a second, and without looking towards Roger or Craig, slowly, almost automatically, placed it on top of one of his piles of mail. He did not lift his head high enough even to see Craig, but spoke to the space ahead of himself — just above Roger's knees.

"When I was the doctor I made rounds every Sunday morning. Under my care no one had bed sores. I was the attending physician, and everyone saw a physician once a week — Sunday morning, the day Jesus rose from the dead. Every nursing home resident has a right to see a doctor once a week. Where's the doctor now? Who cares for these people? Are you going to?"

Roger felt Craig's uncertain look as he stood squarely before Doctor Casparis, wondering how to respond. Roger reached over the doctor, retrieved the envelope and held it sixteen inches from the doctor's face. Craig edged away from the two adults. "Doctor Casparis," Roger spoke loudly, "I am Roger Leeth, the son of Doctor Lester Leeth. He died, but he wanted me to bring you this envelope." The envelope was flimsy, with a lump across the center. Roger wondered if it were a fountain pen, a memento of the early days of writing prescriptions. But Doctor Casparis quickly grabbed the envelope and handled it like a piece of junk mail. He flipped it onto the nightstand. It slid down next to a photograph of two young children.

Roger did not know what to say. Trying to communicate with Doctor Casparis was like the last few months' conversations with Diana. Standing over the aged man he also thought of his father — the person he talked to not at all, a person he did not love or even know well enough to despise. He did not know him at all, nothing about him. This man in the wheelchair might as well be his father. Roger felt nothing for either man; and this one was an inconvenience, an obstacle to overcome before he could get an urn of ashes out of his trunk.

Craig stared at his father. Roger shrugged his shoulders, and bent down, deciding, since Craig was watching the encounter, to try once more and thus leave with a clear conscience. "Doctor Casparis," he was almost shouting into the man's ear as he carefully extracted the envelope so as not to knock over a photograph, "I am Roger Leeth. My father was Doctor Lester Leeth. He died, but he said I was to bring you this envelope. He said that you saved his life and that maybe you could tell me about it." He shoved the letter into the doctor's fragile hand. The doctor held it for a moment, slapped it on his leg, then as a child putting the last block on a tall stack, placed the envelope upon a mound of mail. The room was still. Aged man, middle-aged man, boy: silent. Craig squirmed nervously next to Roger. Doctor Casparis stared between the father and son, eyes focused a thousand yards away. Roger nodded towards the door and they turned to leave. Still focusing his eyes between them Doctor Casparis said, "It was 1966."

"What did you say?"

"1966."

"What was 1966?"

"The last time I saw Les."

Craig and Roger gaped at one another as though being addressed by a ghost.

"We grew up together and both of us moved away, but our folks still lived by one another. We missed each other for years on

96

our trips home, but our folks exchanged information about us and passed it on, so we knew where each other was. In 1966 there was a conference on infectious diseases in Louisville. Through our folks we learned that we'd both be there and planned to meet the first night in the Hyatt Hotel restaurant.

"Les was sitting at a corner table, staring straight ahead, seeing no one go by. I was within two feet before he looked at my body, then up to my face. Took him half a second to recognize me. We hadn't seen each another for almost twenty years. He yelled, 'Frank,' and shook my hand until my shoulder rattled. As soon as we ordered dinner Les was telling about his divorce. Della told him, 'I can't compete with the clinic. I can't sit home waiting for you anymore. I won't go to another concert alone. I won't answer the phone again for you. But you don't have to worry about the kids missing you. They've never known you.' I was shocked, after not having seen Les for a couple decades, for him to rush into his problems as he did. When we were growing up he seldom talked." Roger and Craig looked at each another and nodded. The doctor was definitely talking about the man they knew. "I could not imagine a person as beaten as he was that night, probably weighed 83 pounds — devoid of hope.

"As children we were friends, though not the closest when we were young. We went to church together. In those days kids of all ages were in the same class, not like kids in church today, imprisoned apart by age. One Monday on our way home from school I asked him what he thought of all the church stuff, the Bible and miracles and that. He said, yes, he believed Jesus had come back to life and he trusted that God loved him. He said, 'I've decided to be a medical missionary.' It was because of Les that I believed in God, and I am confident that his studying medicine influenced me later to go to medical school.

"But it was more than that. Les, since he was older than me, protected me as a kid. I was about eight, he around eleven, when some classmates got it in their minds to harass me, call me names during school, chase me after school. When Les saw what was happening we started walking home together. He wasn't much of a fighter, but he slugged a couple of the boys and he took a rock near his temple that was aimed for me, but within a week they stopped it, and we walked home every day for years. As we'd walk I'd ask him about my homework problems and he'd tell me how to figure out the answers. I probably didn't thank him. Kids don't always thank people, but I'm sure I didn't thank him because he did not expect or want it.

"That's what I told him on the night of our reunion. I reminded him of how he not only had protected me, but helped me get through school. One other thing: his family had a lot more money than mine. We were poorer than dirt. That never affected Les and me. In fact — and I told him as he sat there in the corner with his eyes puffy and his cheeks red — I told him how, when we were kids, that he never used his pencils to the nub. He'd use them half way and give them to me, and never in a patronizing way. I told him that I didn't forget it, and that I told my children about him, and that they didn't think of him as Doctor Leeth, but as 'the half pencil doctor.'

"We stayed in the restaurant until they closed at 2 a.m. I finally said, 'Les, if Della doesn't want to be married to you that's her choice. But it's your choice whether to keep practicing medicine. It's what you're good at. It's what God called you to. I'm sorry if Della doesn't agree, but the whole rest of the world does.' I asked him to stay in medicine for another year before making a final decision. I said, 'Will you continue for another year? Whatever you decide I'll honor.' He said he would, and that he'd write to let me know.

"Well, it wasn't a year, it was about fourteen, fifteen months, and I was starting to wonder, but at Christmas an envelope came including only his business card and half a pencil. I wrote back, but he did not respond, until next Christmas: the same message. For 22 years every Christmas, a business card and half a pencil, until nine years ago, he scrawled on the card, 'out of the medical business, but still in business.'

"Thirty-one years, after one conversation over dinner — each Christmas, this present; and he wasn't sending those envelopes to tell me about him. He only mailed the first one for his sake, but the rest were for me. All those years he sent them to encourage me. We both knew which of us needed the most help, and neither of us had to say it. Doctor Lester Leeth was always not only my friend, but my hero, the man who taught me faith and courage, not just when we were kids, but by telling me the truth about his own suffering, allowing me to help when he needed it, and then showing gratitude for the rest of his life."

Doctor Casparis fell silent; then, looking confused, he raised his left arm onto his bed and rubbed the blanket slowly with his hand. His voice became weak, "When I was attending physician I made rounds here on my patients every Sunday morning. No bed sores on any patient. Everyone is a child of God. Every Sunday morning, the day Jesus rose from the dead. Where is the doctor now? Are you the doctor?" He looked toward Roger. "Then you ought to do something. Visit these people. Ask them what they need. Listen to them. Every Sunday morning ..." his voice trailed off. "Every Sunday morning ..." Then, his arm on the bed, his head on his arm, within a minute he slept.

Roger and Craig stood motionless listening to the Doctor breathe. When a cart of lunch trays clattered by, Roger put his arm around Craig and they walked from the room. In the hall Craig said, "Gosh, was he a doctor? Grandpa was a doctor and he never talked, when Doctor Casparis started talking he never stopped!"

They passed a room that did not smell good, and Craig wrinkled his nose and started to walk faster. Roger hurried to catch up with him. "I think the two doctors are a lot alike," Roger said. Craig looked back questioningly. Roger said, "They were both in the habit of saving lives. We'll discuss it again in a few years. I'm pretty sure you'll understand."

But Craig had left the conversation. He pushed open the last door and they stepped out into glaring sunshine. Craig led toward the car, ready for his Walkman. Roger paused to look up at the clearing sky and said, "Yes. A lot alike."

* * *

Our scripture: 1 John 3:18: "Little children, let us love, not in word or speech, but in truth and action." Join with me in prayer.

Let us hold before our loving God those people whom we need to love less with our words and more with our actions ...

Let us hold before God those times and places where we need to stop being concerned about ourselves and begin the habit of saving others' lives ...

Loving God, you have given us the example of your Son Jesus Christ, who loves us when we are not lovable to others, who loves us perfectly in word and speech and in truth and action. May the power of his resurrection lead us into his kind of life, as we join in his habit of saving others. In his name we pray. Amen.

Discussion Questions

Text: 1 John 3:18

1. What immediate responses do you have to the story?

2. If you could have a conversation with one of the characters in this story which would you speak with and what would you ask or say?

3. Do you identify with any character in the story?

4. When is it hardest for you to express love with words?

5. When is it easiest for you to express love by deeds?

6. As a child did you have a hero or heroine who helped your faith?

7. Did you know your childhood heroes or heroines long enough to see them suffer or to see their full humanity?

8. As an adult do you have heroes or heroines? Do you know the people personally, or from afar? How do they help you make your decisions, do your job, or live responsibility in your relationships?

9. In that Christ rewrites our lives, what from this story would you like to have happen in your life?

Chapter 13

Mall Meeting

Joan Detlef slammed the screen door behind her. If the door were real glass instead of plexiglass, it would have shattered all over the front porch. Joan wished it had. She said out loud, "This time it's for good. This time I leave for good." She threw her suitcase in the back seat, slammed the big sedan into reverse, and roared away. She and Bill had stopped yelling half an hour before, but she was still fuming, raging, never so angry in her life. Never so hurt in her life. Never. Bill had retreated from their argument, and simply walked out the back door to the garden to pull weeds. Joan tossed a few clothes into her suitcase. Scribbled on a piece of paper and put it on his pillow, "I'm leaving you."

She drove slapping her right hand hard upon the seat and swearing, then took turns driving with one hand, smashing her other fist into the dashboard and against the steering wheel. She was weeping and screaming as she heard tires screech and a horn honk, and she glanced up to realize that she was running a red light. With one vigorous yank on the wheel she steered her car away from the braking truck on her right. She drove to the curb and parked. She was either hyperventilating or not breathing at all. She was not sure — but she had nearly fainted. She should not be driving, she told herself. Just as bad as driving drunk. Yet she could not go home, and she did not want to go to any of her friends' houses, and she certainly was not comfortable sitting in the car next to an intersection. It made no difference that she had packed her bag. She had left her house being certain only of her departure, not of her destination.

Southgate Mall was three blocks away. Sometimes in the winter when the sidewalks were too dangerous for walking, she and Bill went into the mall "to hoof around," Bill said. So in desperation she drove to the mall's lot, parked, and walked into the building to try to calm her anger by walking. It did not work.

Joan walked as angrily as she drove. Her mind was still back at the house with Bill, arguing with him. They argued over money, always did. For five years they had lived in their new home — new to them, anyway. Built in 1971, it had a beautiful view from the highest hill in town. But that was when and why the arguing began. The house still had its original carpets. The carpets were very good quality, but they were worn now, with the frayed spots and holes covered with a series of throw rugs. Joan wanted new carpets; but Bill had held out for a four-wheel drive pick-up to be able to get up the hill in the icy winters. They never agreed.

Today Bill drove in with a four-wheel drive pick-up. All he said to Joan as she stood open-mouthed was, "We needed it, and Harry offered me his for eleven thousand. It's a better price than I'd get in winter when prices go up for four-wheel drives."

"You what?" Joan had screamed. "My carpet ... " And it went downhill from there. Joan remembered every word: he about practicality instead of beauty, she about home instead of transportation. Joan tramped around the mall, eyes fixed, jaw tight, heels hitting hard every step. "If I ever talk to him again, I'll start by calling him a spoiled child who always wants his own way. That's what I should have said, 'You're a child who wants his toy instead of a husband who cares about his wife.' "

Joan continued her rapid pace, with a fixed stare, noticing no one, only moving mechanically around people in her way, as though everyone was an opposite pole to her magnet.

"Joan." Just ahead of her and to the left was Ann Betteford. Ann grabbed her arm, "Joan, are you all right?"

Joan focused her eyes. She had come to the mall deciding to talk to no one, but here was Ann who had a ghastly look on her face, asking if she was all right. Did Joan look so obviously upset? Ann and Joan were in a discussion class at church, but they did not know one another well. Yet Ann looked so upset by Joan's appearance that she blurted right out, "I'm leaving Bill. I've got my suitcase in the car, but I'm too mad to drive."

She started to cry. Ann looked around. They were standing in front of a coffee shop. She said, "Let's go in and order a cappuccino."

Joan did not answer, just turned and submissively followed the suggestion. As near as either could tell they talked close to two hours with very little coffee drunk. Ann did not say much, merely listened as Joan retold the argument again and again, and explained the five years' recurring disagreements. Ann said, "Uh huh," or "I understand," or "I know what you mean." But that was about it. After an hour Joan began to calm down, partly because anger took so much energy and partly because Ann was so attentive. Ann offered little advice until finally she said, "If I were you, Joan, I'd pray and try talking to Bill again." By that time, Joan had already decided that that was what she would do. And so they parted with a hug and Ann promising to pray for her.

When Joan arrived home she walked through the house and saw Bill still weeding in the garden. Joan did not know what she would say, how to start, how to explain her feelings without attacking Bill. She looked out the window at her husband of thirty years and told herself that yes, she was going to try again.

This was certainly not the end of the problem. But she had a quiet assurance that this would be the beginning toward an end. Before she walked outside to the garden, she went to the bedroom, took from Bill's pillow the paper upon which she'd written, "I'm leaving you," crumpled it, and threw it in the garbage can.

* * *

Twenty-three blocks away Ann Batteford drove into her garage and pressed the remote to close the door behind her. She turned off the engine and sat with her head on her hands on the steering wheel. She was weeping. She had left the house three hours before, shrieking at Jim. She had raced the car down their street with her arms flailing, screaming to the heavens. She had nearly scared herself out of her skin when she had seen that she was driving 45 miles an hour in a residential zone. She was too angry to drive and knew it. Almost disabled by rage she had driven to the mall. Sometimes in the past she had considered shopping as therapy, and maybe now she could walk around and cool down. But she had not. All she could do was replay the fight with Jim, think of the things she should have said, and rehearse what she was going to say, given the chance again.

It came to her that she should pray about her anger, but she frankly admitted to herself that she was too angry to pray. Yet even getting near a prayer is getting near God. That slight thought was a crack through which the breath of God's Spirit blew freshness into her soul. And then she spotted Joan walking towards her, staring off to nowhere, eyes red from crying. Ann had been overcome with Joan's need. No matter what she herself was going through, Ann's heart went out to Joan, all because something had happened in Ann with that small admission that she should pray. The Spirit of the risen Lord Jesus made a frontal assault with love. So Ann found herself responding to the need of another person and forgetting about her own difficulties. Within her was the Spirit of Jesus; and thus, no matter the circumstances, she now lived as he lived, putting the needs of others above her own.

Jesus did it naturally; it was his nature, every day, as predictable as law. Maybe he could not have stopped himself if he had tried. He would love and care for others and trust God to care for him no matter how bad the circumstances. It was so much who Jesus was that on the cross he did the same thing — cared for others more than himself. It is what his entire life and death were about.

Therefore, Ann, walking in the mall or sitting in her car in the garage, was overcome by someone whose love was so strong it can change us from being concerned only about ourselves to being concerned about others, whose love helps us trust God to take care of us no matter how difficult the situation.

Ann prayed for Joan and Bill as she promised she would, then finally and fully prayed for Jim and herself. She retrieved her suitcase from the back seat, got out of the car, and entered the house to look for Jim and try again. She had practiced, and been changed for having done so, what Paul the apostle told the Galatian churches about the Christian lifestyle: "Bear one another's burdens, and in this way you will fulfill the law of Christ."

Discussion Questions

Text: Galatians 6:1-2

1. What immediate responses do you have to the story?

2. If you could have a conversation with one of the characters in this story, which would you speak with and what would you ask or say?

3. Do you identify with any character in the story?

4. Have you been incapacitated by anger? Are you normally angry? What do you usually do to release your anger in a constructive way?

5. How do you feel in the company of angry people? Can you listen to other people's anger without excusing or condemning it?

6. Have you been helped by someone who needed as much help as you did?

7. Have you helped when you believed your resources for helping were depleted?

8. In that Christ rewrites our lives, what from this story would you like to have happen in your life?

Chapter 14

Life Beside The Falls

The first storm of autumn clamped down with unseasonable cold — lows at night in the teens — which turned the shores of the falls in the middle of town to parallel strips of white lace. Despite the frozen ground the season's last football game would be played, swirls of snow sometimes making the players invisible from the stands. The teams warmed up on the field, stretching and shouting numbers to the rhythm of their exercises. The band members tuned their instruments, the public address announcer counted through the speakers as fans filed into the shelter of the stadium. Phil and I shouldered into the wind, Phil maneuvering the wheelchair toward the stands. Slowly he pushed and turned the chair, and Millie — heavily robed and blanketed — bobbed side to side with every bump.

Millie Freeman was a native of this town which had the descriptive but not very imaginative name of Falls, for the waterfall which neatly divided the town in half. She was born Mildred Dodson in 1910, the year the water-powered grist mill was finally torn down. The town had grown around the mill, then the mill stood vacant and crumbling for a generation until finally it was razed. Born into a town of 1100, by the time Millie was limited to a wheelchair Falls was a city of 63,000.

Mildred was never pretty. She would say, "But I don't have to look at me." Yet she was startling for her height and erect posture. For her generation she was tall — six feet, one inch. Besides her height and erect carriage, her only outstanding physical feature was a nose too long for her narrow face.

A space awaited the wheelchair, but getting into the stands took us time and effort — shifting and dragging sideways. Millie sat silently in her chair, almost expressionless. She was chilled already.

When finally in her place, we left her alone. She would have it no other way. The game began and although we stood to yell or slapped our gloved hands to stay warm, Millie sat motionless, head bent forward.

Mildred had always wanted children, desired children more than she desired marriage. The happiest moment in her life was not when she married Harold Freeman — dear man that he was — but when she gave birth to her first child, Henry. Then her happiest moment was when she birthed Marshall, and so also with Leona and Martha. Mildred said, "Parents are allowed multiple most happiest moments."

Mildred's most happiest moments all had to do with her children. That's how I met Mildred — through her youngest daughter, Martha. Martha Freeman and I, Margaret Fest, were best friends from thirteen until we graduated from high school and left for separate colleges. Mildred and Harold's other three children called Martha and me the "Nutty M & M's."

For all the time I spent at the Freemans' home, it took a year or so to get used to Mildred. Mildred said, "I'm not a milk-and-cookies mother." She seemed stern when she made clear what I could and could not do while visiting or when she sent word it was time for me to leave or for Martha to come home. And Mildred was so tall; but I grew comfortable with Mrs. Freeman because I could ask anything and get a straight answer. Mildred's yeses were always pleasing and it proved painless when she said, "No."

Since Mildred's life goal was to be a mother, she helped at school and attended her children's every play, concert, academic presentation, and athletic contest. Her children would bring home the announcement of another school event and Mildred would say, "I'll be there." Being a mother was the most important activity of her life. That's why her quandary when Martha, her last child, started school. "What will I do all day if I don't have a child around the house?" Harold encouraged her not to get a job so she could be home when the children returned from school. She began her hunt for a hobby. All that autumn she fiddled, trying to crochet, then cross-stitch, then embroider. It was not a pleasant fall for the rest of the family as they would come home to find Mildred angrily trying to be creative. Finally after one day of knitting she informed her family at supper she was going to write, every day, from eleven in the morning until one in the afternoon.

Harold asked, "Write what?"

"I don't know, but I'll write."

Martha wondered, "Who you going to write to, Mommy?"

"Good question. I think I'll start by writing to me."

Martha told me that she did not understand. None of the family understood; but they were wise enough to say no more. The next day Mildred was at the table in the kitchen at 11 a.m., a can of pencils, a stack of paper, a large pink rubber eraser, and a dictionary in front of her. Mildred had done enough with her hands for years; here at the table she set out to do something with her brain, to write letters as she had to her grandparents, to write essays as she produced for the high school newspaper, to write poems as she did when she met Harold.

The first night Harold and the kids walked into the kitchen and looked at the table. They could not see much sign of writing. A week passed with little discussion of the daily project, then a month; however, Mildred did not say a lot about what she did for two hours in the middle of every day. The children told their friends at school and the practice seemed quite strange to us all. But Mildred wrote, wrote letters to friends, wrote poems and prayers and stories, started a drama. To her greatest liking was the essay. She wrote seven months until she decided she wanted to direct her thought through essays; because there she could ask questions and come up with answers. She said, "Meaning has to be sought and struggled for." Thus in essays she reflected upon what happened in the family, neighborhood, or town and discovered what it meant in the larger scheme of life. Through essays she investigated life, probed past the obvious, asked questions, and found out why.

I had just become a friend of Martha's when the long trauma began over football. Henry wanted to go out for the high school football team, but Mildred refused. Harold disagreed with her, but not in front of the children. "Millie, when Hank says other boys get to play football, he's right. He's a strong boy. I think he should get to play."

"No, I can't allow our children to risk an injury that could disable them. I know it's hard for Hank and everybody, but I can't bear to have my child in a game that could ruin his health for life."

It was difficult for Harold, as well as for Henry, but knowing how Mildred loved the children, Harold agreed and held out against Henry. The more difficult problem followed next year with Marshall. Henry was an average athlete, but Marshall was a star at every sport. He knew his abilities, and all the coaches in high school had been waiting for him. Yet Mildred stuck to the same conclusion for the same reasons. Neither temper nor tears availed, and Marshall's high school years, and his relationship with his mother, were darkened by the confrontations.

A year after she began her daily discipline of writing, she approached the newspaper editor for a weekly column, but he refused. So Mildred went back to her desk and continued writing essays and articles, and when she submitted them to newspapers elsewhere her copy was often accepted. When a new editor arrived in town she showed up in his office with a stack of her clippings and he agreed to try her out. By the time of the football controversies Mildred was writing her weekly column, "Life Beside the Falls." She commented upon some thought or occurrence, a happening in town, visitors, the weather, accidents, awards, the seasons. "It's all grist for the mill," she said, quoting her father. Under her careful eye the small happenings in town gained greater significance, as she asked what this event meant and why that happened, and then made her decision and gave an opinion from her philosophy or faith. For decades she never missed a deadline, not even when Harold died at 74, though his death noticeably changed the mood of her writing. At the end of each column she signed off as though she had just written a personal letter to everyone in town:

"Until next week,

Mildred Dodson Freeman."

Her eightieth birthday became the day to submit her last column. The newspaper, along with the downtown merchants, had a party for her. She had written her way through four and a half editors and was their newspaper's oldest employee — in age and seniority. I drove Mildred to the party. Mildred and I had met together every Thursday (deadline was Wednesday) since I moved back to town with my husband, Phillip Frazer, our son, Robbie, and daughter, Jessica. Six months before Harold died I had shown up at the Freeman's door — the first people I visited upon returning. My parents had moved away years before; now, 25 years after leaving for college, I returned to the town where I graduated from high school.

Thirteen months after Mildred retired from the paper, Phillip and I helped her move from her house to an apartment. Then late the next summer on a Thursday I knocked on Mildred's door. When she answered, the room was full of smoke and she was shaking, "I put a pan on the burner and forgot it."

"Here, Millie, I'll help you clean up. It's okay." I put my arm around her. "Just settle down; it could happen to anyone."

Millie was trying to stop shaking, "It's the third time I've done it this week — or a week or two. And yesterday I found a stack of bills I haven't paid, some are past due. I'm forgetting things all the time, important things. I have to move to assisted living."

"No, Millie, you'll move in with us."

Millie looked seriously into my face, "I couldn't do that, Maggie. You've got your family."

"No, Millie, you'll move in with Phil and me and the kids."

"I have the money to pay for a place. There's no reason for me ..."

"No, Millie, you'll move in with us."

She wiped a tear from her narrow face, "All right, but I'll bother you as little as possible. I'll help all I can, and I'll pay you."

"That's fine."

So began an unexpected adventure between the generations, because Millie moved into Robbie's room and he had to take the smaller room that had been his father's office. Jessica got to keep her room. A month later Robbie, a freshman in high school, began the daily doubles of football practice. To Robbie, Millie came into the home famous for her resistance to football. So Robbie and Millie didn't say much to one another. Phil and I waited and watched. Robbie made the Varsity, and the night arrived for his first home game. It was my place to bring up the subject, "Millie, we're going to Robbie's football game. We'll be leaving around seven; be home after nine."

"I'll go with you."

Thus it went for four years. Only when asked did Millie complain, "It's a game I neither understand nor enjoy." But every home game she slowly made her way into the stands. For two seasons she was able to make it with a cane, then she had to use a walker, and finally, in Robbie's senior year she was confined to a wheelchair; but she went without discussion.

Other games had been brutally cold, but tonight was the worst. It was the last of Robbie's senior year, and a state playoff berth hung on the results. The dry snow eddied and skimmed over the field and through the players. First downs, quarters, and scores came and went unheeded by Millie. Occasionally a snowflake landed on her face and melted slowly. Phil and I sat near. Jessica was in the student section. Millie was bowed, nose dripping, lips blue. She could not break old mental habits. She was asking herself about the game and her presence there. She questioned the night and the place. In her mind she pushed meaning into carefully crafted sentences, not for her column of the week, but for the column of her life.

Saturday, off and on, she typed in her bedroom; and Sunday morning at breakfast she gave me this piece. "A good morning gift," she said. "I want you to have this before my *final* deadline."

"What does it mean to be here — an old lady swaddled like a seated mummy, at a frozen football game, in this city beside the falls? What conclusions can be drawn by a person who has lived 86 years in a town split in half by water? Are we who live in Falls better equipped to understand life than those who do not have a river falling through their village?

"Perhaps the river that divides our town is the stream the prophet Ezekiel saw flowing out from God's temple, beside the altar and into the whole land. Maybe that is the source of every river, making wholesome all the land and people through which it flows.

"It cascades through our world and community as through the two halves of our soul, to teach us we are part of something larger than ourselves, that we came from somewhere and go somewhere.

Since it is God's river it instructs us that God's highest purpose for human beings is fulfilled when we grow and mature in loving one another; and it is best to err on the side of loving too much.

"It is in our daily living that our loyalties, as a river, wear away rocks. We make our mistakes and try again. We give and forgive. We make and keep promises, endure pains and sacrifices, and are forced into compromises. But this is the goal set before us as humans — care more for others than for ourselves, no matter the cost, and trust that the great creator of all rivers shall carry us away at the right time, and life will somehow be better for our having lived here.

"Until next, ... well, just 'until,'
Mildred Dodson Freeman."

Discussion Questions

Text: Ezekiel 47:1-12

1. What immediate responses do you have to the story?

2. If you could have a conversation with one of the characters in this story which would you speak with and what would you ask or say?

3. Do you identify with any character in the story?

4. Do you have a controlling image or vision that explains life to you?

5. Where do you believe God is filling your world with life? Where is the Spirit flowing in your life? What is the river of God refreshing, renewing, or repairing right now in your life? What is greening up for you, starting or starting over?

6. In that Christ rewrites our lives, what from this story would you like to have happen in your life?

www.ingramcontent.com/pod-product-compliance
Lightning Source LLC
LaVergne TN
LVHW021523080426
835509LV00018B/2628